Quality of Work Life
In
Commercial Banks

Quality of Work Life In Commercial Banks

Edited by

Dr. B. Anitha
M.B.A., Ph.D.
Sri Krishnadevaraya Institute of Management
S.K. University, Anantapur—515 003
(Andhra Pradesh)

Prof. P. Subba Rao
M.Com., Ph.D.
Sri Krishnadevaraya Institute of Management
S.K. University, Anantapur—515 003
(Andhra Pradesh)

DISCOVERY PUBLISHING HOUSE
NEW DELHI - 110 002

ISBN: 978-81-7141-431-4

Quality of Work Life in Commercial Banks

Published by:
DISCOVERY PUBLISHING HOUSE PVT. LTD.
4383/4B, Ansari Road, Darya Ganj
New Delhi-110 002 (India)
Phone: +91-11-23279245, 43596064-65
Fax: +91-11-23253475
E-mail: discoverypublishinghouse@gmail.com
sales@discoverypublishinggroup.com
web: www.discoverypublishinggroup.com

Printed at:
Infinity Imaging Systems
Delhi

Preface

Human Resource is an important factor of production whose behaviour and productivity cannot be predicted. As such management of human resource is a complex process. However, productivity can be improved considerably through proper management of human resources. Proper management of human resource play a significant role in developing countries like ours. Proper human resource management depends on various factors, including Quality of Work Life.

The changing needs of employees, their culture, values, aspirations and work environment give birth to new sub-systems of human resource management. One such new sub-system is Quality of Work Life (QWL). The concept 'Quality of Work Life' appeared in research journals in 1970s for the first time. But this concept was given potential importance right from 1950s. Quality of Work Life can be said as work culture of the Organisation, as pointed out by Richard Walton. It comprises whole work life of employee at the organisations. As such, such work culture is to be identified and improved in order to improve Quality of Work Life. QWL covers many aspects of employee's work life such as monetory benefits, physical working conditions, social and career aspects.

QWL has its initial roots in scientific management. It took a shape with human relations movement and it is socio-technical system, which forms the basis for present QWL.

Measures for improvement of QWL are practised in many western countries like U.S.A., Great Britain, Sweden, Italy, and West Germany.

Though Prof. Rice found basis for QWL with his studies on QWL in Calico Mills, Ahmedabad along with famous Touvi-stock Studies, India is slow in adopting practices to improve QWL for various reasons. In fact, improvement of QWL has gained importance only recently. Government influence in this regard is minimum. The inclusion of workers participation in management did not influence much the improvement of QWL.

Many authors and researches advocated various criterion for measurement of QWL. Improving QWL is possible only with the measurement of existing QWL. But the eight-point criteria advocated by Richard Walton is still being considered as most effective and feasible. These eight points cover all important aspects of employee work life.

What is important at this stage is developing QWL consciousness among all parties of industry, i.e., workers, unions and management. Only with this realisation do these parties strive towards improvement which results in worker's satisfaction.

QWL plays pivotal role in service industries like commercial banks. Commercial banks form an important part of service organisations. In India, where the country is marching towards revamping economic structure through liberalisation policies, the commercial banks are expected to play a crucial and vital role.

Human Resource Management is more complex in service - oriented industries as they deal with rendering services directly. Complexities of human resource management in service organisations may be reduced to some extent by improving QWL. As such efforts should be taken to improve the QWL and thereby productivity.

Studies on QWL in India are limited. But the studies on QWL in commercial banks are rare to find. Hence, an attempt is made to study the QWL in commercial banks. Two banks—one from public sector i.e., Andhra Bank and another from private sector (largest among private sector) i.e., The Vysya Bank Ltd., are selected for the study.

The study confines to the existing state of QWL by measuring it through eight-point criteria advocated by Richard Walton.

Present study focuses the concept 'Quality of Work Life' in Chapter 1. Chapter 2 is devoted to examine the growth and development of commercial banks in general and profiles of Andhra Bank and the Vysya Bank Ltd., in particular. Research methodology of the study is presented in Chapter 3. The economic aspects of QWL are presented in Chapter 4 and Human Resource Development aspects of Quality of Work Life are discussed in Chapter 7. Evaluation of all these aspects and suggestions to improve QWL in respondent commercial banks are presented in Chapter 8.

Dr. B. Anitha
Prof. P. Subba Rao

Acknowledgement

We would like to acknowledge some of the people who have made major contribution to this book. We relayed heavily on the comments and suggestions of our colleagues in S.K. Institute of Management. We want to express our thanks to Prof. Ch. Rama Prasad Rao and Dr. Murali Krishna who were especially helpful and to all other colleagues.

The Management and employees of Andhra Bank and the Vysya Bank Ltd. were very co-operative. Our deepest thanks goes to them.

Finally, we would like to acknowledge the support extended by our families who were deprived of our attention for an year.

Dr. B. Anitha
Prof. P. Subba Rao

Contents

Preface v

Acknowledgement ix

1. Quality of Work Life 1
2. Evolution and Growth of Andhra Bank and The Vysya Bank Ltd. 27
3. Research Design 47
4. Economic Aspects of Quality of Work Life 58
5. Working Conditions 72
6. Social Aspects of Quality of Work Life 83
7. Human Resource Development Aspects of Quality of Work Life 105
8. Evaluation and Suggestions 125

Bibliography 145

1

Quality of Work Life

Introduction

Economic, social and cultural development of any country mostly depends upon the human resource it has. According to Arthur Lewis, "there are great differences in development between countries which seem to have roughly equal resources, so it is necessary to enquire into the difference in human behaviour".[1] As such though the countries are endowed with same level of natural resources, technology and international aid etc., their productivity and development mostly depends upon the availability of efficient human resource and more importantly, commitment of such resource.

Internationalisation of both public and private sector organisations has rapidly changed the complexion of human resource management. The internationalisation of organisation makes human resource management more challenging because it raises a number of new issues[2] like cross-cultural training, compensation and benefits etc. As such the human resource should be viewed with an international perspective.

Another recent development that has taken place is shifting importance from manufacturing to service-oriented organisations which has resulted in growing importance of the human resource. Without predicting human behaviour at a particular point of the time and guiding them in proper direction, service organisations cannot survive and prosper.

Efficient human resource and their commitment is essential for effective management of organisation. The management of four

Ms i.e., Money, Materials, Machines and Men is essentially carried on by human resource of the organisation. Stressing this point of view, McGregor observed that effectiveness of organisations would be doubled if managements could discover how to tap the unrealised potential present in their human resources.[3]

The depreciation that results in all other factors of production in long run doesn't result in case of human resource. In fact, vice versa is true. Human resources with proper organisation and motivation can grow and develop their potential in long run. There is no depreciation value for human resource. Stressing this, Peter. F. Druckur remarked that man, of all resources available to man, can grow and develop.[4] As such deriving maximum potentialities from this resource largely depends upon proper management of it.

It is said that, "behaviour of human beings differs widely. It is in turn very difficult to predict their behaviour, especially in organisations where they work in groups. Their behavior is neither consistent nor predictable. Thus the manager should recognise that individuals not organisations, create excellence."[5]

Most of the complexities in modern organisations arise from human behaviour. It is human resource which can make a difference and which can have an everlasting impact of the survival of any organisation. In this context, Oliver Sheldon observed that, "no industry can be rendered efficient so long as the basic fact remains unrecognised that it is principally human. It is not a mass of machines and technical processes but a body of men. It is not a complex of matter, but a complex of humanity. It fulfills its functions, not by virtue of some impersonal force, but by human energy. Its body is not an intricate maze of mechanical device but a magnified nervous system".[6] Human resources should be handled carefully by predicting the behaviour to the possible extent, in view of the complexities involved in managing them.

Directing human resource of an organisation is guiding entire organisation towards stand objectives. Because organising any functional area is in turn organising and leading human resource of that functional area. Organisation is nothing but collection of human resource who takes up various functions to attain set objectives. "Thus all executives must unavoidably be personnel managers".[7]

Although the human resource is a sub-system of an organisation, it affects all other sub-systems and entire organisation in turn. Wendell L. French rightly puts it, "Personnel management is a major pervasive sub-system of all organisation".[8]

Human resource management consists of many sub-systems like training and development, compensation, industrial relations etc. Human resource management concerns itself regarding employee right from recruitment till his retirement. Human resource management takes care of inducting suitable human resource into the organisation through recruitment and selection, sharpen and enrich their capabilities and skills through training and development, motivates and provides welfare through compensation and maintain good relations and atmosphere inside the organisation through maintaining good industrial relations in the organisation. Many new sub-systems are being added to human resource management with the changing needs of employees, their culture, expectations and work environment.

One such new area is 'Quality of Work Life". The term "Quality of Work Life' appeared in research journals only in 1970s. It is not only monetary aspects that a modern employee concerns himself with. His is also concerned with conditions of employment, interpersonal conflicts, role conflicts, job pressure, lack of freedom of work and absence of challenging work etc. As the style of management has changed from paternalistic to democratic, so as the expectations of employees with an impending need to achieve more and more productivity efficiently, employees look forward to the conductive and congenial working conditions and favorable terms of employment. As such productivity and efficiency of an organisation largely depends upon the quality of work life provided by the organisation.

Quality of Work Life—Past and Present

"Blessed is he, who has found his work. Let him ask no other blessedness. It is work and only work which changes the individual, the society and nation",[9] was the comment of Carlyle in his 'Past and Present'. Such is the importance of the work in one's life. Work is a major aspect of life that it influences one's life-style tremendously.

Rosow (1974) explains the importance of work more in detail and relates it to success and failure of a man in his society. According to him, "Work is the core of life considering the deeper meaning of work to be individual and to life's values; work means being a good provider; it means autonomy; it pays off in success, and it establishes self-respect or self-worth. Within this framework, the person who openly confesses active job dissatisfaction is virtually admitting failure as a man, a failure in fulfilling his moral role in society".[10]

Though concept "Quality of Work Life" appeared in print only in 1970 in USA, the concept with being given potential importance right from early 1950s. But it was not very clear and was ambiguous. 'Quality of Work Life' is interpreted and viewed in different ways. The term continues to be vague though many people tried to define it in specific terms. A few among them are presented below.

Richard Walton (1979) who had taken up extensive research on Quality of Work Life made significant contribution for the conceptualisation of the team Quality of Work Life. In fact, measuring QWL has become easy and practicable with the factors/elements that he proposed. According to Walton, "Quality of Work Life is the work culture that serves as the corner stone".[11] Hence, work culture of an organisation should be recognised and improved to improve Quality of Work Life of that Organisation.

Robert F. Craver, a senior executive at AT & T on the other hand views : "QWL is more than a fad, more than an attempt to pacify the growing demands of impatient employees. For the manager, QWL can offer new challenges, opportunities for growth and satisfaction."[12]

Robert H.Guest, a noted behavioral scientist talks about feelings of an employee about his work while defining Quality of Work Life. He further points out the effect of QWL on person's life. According to him, "QWL is a generic phrase that covers a person's feelings about every dimension of work, including economic rewards and benefits, security, working conditions, organisational and interpersonal relationships, and its intrinsic meaning in a person's life", and "It is a process by which an Organisation attempts to unlock the creative potential of its people by involving them in decisions affecting their work lives."[13]

In the development process, the term QWL has acquired many different definitions creating confusion. Nadler and Lawler (1983) brought out this confusion thus—

Definition of QWL

First definition	1969-1972	Qwl	=	Variable
Second definition	1969-1975	QWL	=	Approach
Third definition	1972-1975	QWL	=	Methods
Fourth definition	1975-1980	QWL	=	Movement
Fifth definition	1969-1982	QWL	=	Everything[14]

Whatever may be the interpretation, QWL is most debated topic both by employers and employees. One of the reasons for its growing importance could be realisation on the part of employees about their rights and growing unionism. Workers are no more illiterate. They do not completely depend upon the mercy of management for their existence. Most of the lower level workers also have atleast primary education. Thanks to the efforts of the Governments in this regard. Each and every worker tends to join some union or the other for his own protection and well-being. Unions putting all their efforts to educate their members to realise their rights and as to what they expect from management in return of what they contribute. Though still monetary benefits occupy the first place in the list of elements of QWL, other elements like physical working conditions, job restructuring and redesign, career development, promotional opportunities etc., are gaining importance rapidly. As such the workers expect management to improve QWL by providing all these facilities.

The Management on the other hand, ceased to adopt paternalistic approach as it used to earlier. They do not take care of the employee as a parent takes care of his child. There is no more understanding between employer and employee, except constant struggle for their own end. Employer always sees the employees as a factor of production just like other factors. He always tries to extract as much production as possible from this factor, whereas the employees always expect more facilities and comforts from employer in return to what they contribute. This situation has resulted in constant struggle between employees and employers.

QWL emerged to end such exploitation and injustice on the part of the employers. As De (1976) pointed out, "QWL is an indicator of how free the society is from exploitation, injustice, inequality, oppression and restrictions on the continuity of growth of man, leading to his development to the fullest."[15]

Apart from the above problems, there are other serious problems cropping up, like job dissatisfaction due to meaningless, repetitive or irrelevant jobs or authoritarian behaviour of the boss. As a result counterproductive behaviour like absenteeism, idling while on work and lack of concentration takes place.

Because of poor design of socio-technical system, employees also experience alienation. Alienation is a feeling of powerlessness, lack of meaning, loneliness, boredom, lack of ego involvement and lack of attachment to job.[16] This job discontent and job pressures may inturn affect employees' health giving way to general unhappiness. Hence, it is viewed that QWL should be designed along with all activities of Human Resource Amusement as given in the following examples.

HR activity	Effect on QWL
Job Analysis	Analyse the job in such a way that human needs like freedom, challenging work, autonomy can be satisfied.
Selection	Selecting the right man and placing him in the right position. This satisfies his needs for reward, interesting work etc.
Job Enrichment	Satisfy higher order needs like pride and ego.
Job Evaluation	Equitable wages. [17]

QWL has its roots in scientific management advocated by F.W. Taylor in the sense that, the mechanical/quantitative approach that the scientific management assumed gave way to frustration of the workers which led to human relations movement and later socio-technical movement which was the basis for today's Quality of Work Life.

Thus the evolution of the concept QWL was mainly in 3 phases—scientific management movement, human relations movement and finally socio-technical movement. Federick W. Taylor (1947) was the advocate of scientific management movement. As a result of industrial revolution, there arised a great need to increase productivity of work organisations. Taylor, in an attempt to achieve this, came up with the idea of scientific management, time study and work study. He viewed that the burden of planning and designing the work should be removed from the shoulders of workers. They should be given specific tasks and clear instructions as to how a particular job should be done before hand. He also advocated 'Division of Work' which means that instead of assigning a worker entire job, divide it into parts and assign each part to a different worker. As such each worker will have to do only a part of total job, thus specialising in that work. Taylor hoped that such specialisation would quicken the production process. He further advocated various incentive schemes which would enable a worker a who achieves a particular level of production, to earn certain percentage of incentive.

With the help of time, work and motion studies, Taylor viewed that workers can be briefed exactly what is to be done, when, where and how, leaving practically nothing to their discretion. Taylor had put his thoughts in point in his work "The principles of scientific management" in 1911 which was the most popular work of that period and influenced not only the American industry, but industry all over the world for atleast quarter of the century.

Taylor, through his time and work study, division of labour, and incentive schemes, tried to improve work life of employees. Through incentive scheme and division of labour Taylor contributed towards Quality of Work Life.

Fayol was another pioneer of similar approach with his 14 principles. But he concentrated on general management unlike Taylor who concentrated his research only on shop floor management. Fayol tried to improve QWL through some of his principles like division of work, unity of command and direction, remuneration and esprit de corps.

Taylor's work was most popular as well as most criticised one. Production levels started increasing with the application of principles of scientific management. But elimination of human element by Taylor started showing its effect soon. Industrial unrest began to rise as a result of repetitive work and rigid standards prescribed to the workers. The general feeling among workers was that the best judges on to how and when to do their work is they themselves and not supervisors or managers. They further felt that with their sole objective of increasing the production, the managers tend to set-up strict and rigid standards which cannot be reached always by an average worker. Lack of apathy on the part of employers drove workers to think that they were being cheated and exploited. The application of incentive schemes only worsened their human relations. A quick and skilled worker could earn more whereas a below average worker couldn't even earn normal wages as there were standards to be reached to earn normal wages. This resulted in groupism, back-biting and spoiled the general environment of the Organisation. The workers attributed all this to scientific management.

Not only was Taylor targeted to the criticism of workers, but also, other groups like academicians, researchers, and anthropologists. They felt that Taylor considered human beings as just another factor of production. He fixed standards, time limits and work schedules to workers as they do to machines. As such Taylor's was mainly mechanical approach. This negative approach towards human beings was criticised.

As the realisation of human potential grew, criticism on scientific management grew. This resulted researches in thinking more about human approach in the industry. The industrial unrest and constant bickering among management and workers also stressed the need to think a different approach which can overcome the drawbacks of scientific management and give due recognition and importance to human element, which finally resulted in 'Human Relations Movement'.

Human Relations Movement

Human relations movement was mainly concerned with inter-personal and group relationships among workers and advocated a participatory and democratic style of supervision to achieve work effectiveness. Maslow (1954), Herzberg (1959) and McGregor (1960) were all importance members of Human Relations school who contributed towards this view.

Quality of work life has its roots in the theories of Moslow, Herzbeg and Mc Gregor. The need for fulfillment as that of Abraham

Maslow's motivational theory of need hierarchy are comparable with those of the factors of QWL. Basic needs like monetary benefits come first, with good working conditions following. Later comes career planning, growth and development of human capabilities to satisfy. Moslow's esteem needs are comparable with opportunity to use and develop human capabilities. Lastly challenging work is advocated by Walton to satisfy self-actualisation need in need hierarchy. Quality of work life concerns itself with satisfying both hygiene factors and motivators as identified by Herberg to improve the work life of employees. The assumptions of McGregor can be divided into two sets i.e., those under, 'Theory *x*' and those under 'Theory *y*' gave realisation of changing attitudes, values and work culture of employees. Quality of work life assumes that all employees basically belongs to 'Theory Y'. Thus, it is evidence that the QWL has had its origin in these theories of motivation.

Socio-Technical System

An improved school of thought from Human Relations movement is socio-technical system which forms actual basis for present Quality of Work Life.

The Tavistock Institute of Human Relations (1947) conducted a series of studies in coal mines. There was a subsequent research in Calico Textile Mills in Ahmedabad which was conducted by Prof. A. K. Rice. These two studies form basis for socio-technical movement.

The basic feature of socio-technical system is—"The design of the organisation must be compatible with its objectives. In order to adopt to change and be capable of using the creative capacities of the individual a system should be provided to the people that gives an opportunity to participate in the design of the jobs they are required to perform."[18] as Cherns (1979) puts it.

The objectives should be specific. But specification of tasks, allocation of tasks to jobs or jobs to roles, specification of methods of obtaining them should be minimum. The employees, given specific objectives, should be able to plan and design their own activities. There should also be variance control i.e., the employees should be able to recheck and insect their own work. This enables them to learn from their own mistakes.

The role of supervisors should be confined to boundary activities like ensuring resources to the employer, co-ordinating with other departments and forecasting likely changes and informing them to the employees etc.

The organisational design should ensure high quality of Work Life. The six psychological requirements of working people, which were advocated by Emery and Thorsord (1969), should be taken care while designing the organisation. These factors are :[19]

(i) The need for variety of content of a job (not necessarily novelty).

(ii) The need for being able to learn on the job and to go on learning.

(iii) The need for some minimal area of decision-making that the individual can call his own.

(iv) The need for some minimal degree of social support and recognition in the work place.

(v) The need for individual to be able to relate what he does and what he produces to his social life.

(vi) The need to feel that the job leads to some sort of desirable future.

No organisation is independent social or independent technical system. Organization is an interdependent social and technical system. Socio-technical system require social and technical system to be jointly optimised. It is from this notion of socio-technical system that the 'Quality of Work Life' emerged.

QWL—India—Abroad

Experiments are being conducted in industrially advanced countries to find out cause of general frustration among employees and resulting misunderstandings between management and employees and the ultimate industrial sickness and unrest.

The famous Tavistock studies from which socio-technical system emerged provided answers to most of these questions. In brief, this system advocated industrial democracy, participative management, minimum involvement of management in the tasks of employees and improved interpersonal relations to overcome the labour problems. Managements, especially in industrially developed countries were quick to react to these suggestions. As such they had taken up research and experimental studies in their organisations. With good results showing up in no time, these organisations started practicing the same.

The employees also, being more educated and more informed through unions, grew more logical and demanded for increased involvement in the management.

Though the studies conducted in Calico Mills Limited, Ahmedabad by Rice found basis for QWL along with Tavistock studies, India is slow in adopting socio-technical system and improving QWL. The reasons are :

(i) The people in India generally are unadoptive to anything which is new. Initial resistance is evident in adopting anything which is new, no matter how it improves the ability of the organisation. The management tend to stick on to the traditional methods of getting work done from the employees. As such they did not take any measures to improve QWL for a long time.

(ii) The employees of the workers in India are also not educated in general. They do not have much logical power. There is also a tendency as said earlier to stick on to the old rather that adopt something new. Some of the unions even felt the measures for improving quality of work life by the management is nothing but getting more work done by the workers with no major costs.

(iii) Improving Quality of Work Life also involves considerable amount to be spent by the management. The employers were initially hesitant to spend. This has given negative attitude to employees.

But the scene has changed. Now, both management and workers are realising the importance of QWL. In fact, QWL has become a buzzword in the industries these days and even laymen talk about it. Let us examine practices of QWL in some of the industrially advanced countries and proceed to discuss the present situation in India in this regard.

United States of America

Quality of work life is sometimes referred to as humanising

the working life and emphasising the human factor. USA can be said as pioneer in developing thoughts, ideas and identifying various dimensions of QWL. Richard E.Walton, an American professor played a major role in developing the concept of Quality of Work Life. In fact, the eight factors that he proposed to measure QWL made the task easy worldwide. Still these factors are mostly used in measuring QWL.

The experience of the famous General Motors has to be presented while discussing QWL in USA. General Motors had to face labour problems like high ratio of absenteeism and labour turnover and also high costs of operations. The employee-employer relations were marred with fear and mistrust. On the whole environment was not healthy and the productivity rapidly declined. The management was worried and desired a solution. Finally, they decided to launch QWL programme involving 3800 workers and supervisors. This programme emerged from an agreement between the United Auto Workers' Union (Union) and the General Motors in 1973.

The actual programme was started in 1977 with the objectives of developing the concept of QWL:

i) Determining plans and functions of both Management and Union; and

ii) Acquiring problem solving skills.

This programme which was initially started at Tarrytown plan gave excellent results like improved productivity, improved product quality and also improved labour-management relations. This success made General Motors practise the same programme throughout its plants which produce outstanding results. Today, the world's largest car manufacturing organisation still practices QWL programmes with designing new plant to practise socio-technical system.

The success story of General Motors itself talks about future QWL in USA. Other major organisations like Ford and Chrysler, have taken up QWL improvement programmes.

National agreement between United Steel workers and the largest companies had also given similar results, if not better. This agreement establishment labour-management participation teams in selected plants which is a strategy to improve QWL.

Another experience is that American Telephone and Telegraph Company (AT & T). AT & T made an agreement with communications workers of America in early 1980s, with a massive involvement of about half a million workers. Some of the interesting points which came out in a subsequent survey were:

— Union leaders felt that QWL improvement projects require them to gain new skills and knowledge.

— Union leaders also felt that intra-union rivalry may delay the process.

— Both management and Unions felt that projects such as this require team-work, trust and co-ordination.

— They also felt that QWL-improvement programmes are meant to strengthen their organisation.

— Over 80 per cent of employees volunteered to participate in the programme.

Quite a few Federal Agencies like National Centre for Productivity and Quality of Working Life as well as some of the private organisations like American Quality of Work Centre are working towards spreading and developing the concept of QWL. There are also research programmes going on in noted universities and management institutes.

The United Kingdom

The very basis of QWL is in UK in the sense that the Tavistock Institute of Human Relations, U.K., carried out research into what they called as socio-technical system from which the concept of QWL emerged.

Changing economic environment due to the impact of world war and changing technology, changing political environment due to increased Government intervention brought in changes in industrial scene of the country, which initiated improved co-operation and trust between management and workers, which paved way for practices of QWL.

Shell UK Ltd., launched QWL programmes in its microwave department to overcome impending labour problems like low-morals, high cost and poor maintenance. Restructuring of job tasks was done and more decision-making power was given to the employees. This had provided for improvement of QWL which paid back in terms of 50 per cent decline in absenteeism, 75 per cent reduction off plant testing line and 70 per cent increase in output.

The sales level was increased by 18 per cent in ICI with the introduction of a system of more autonomy and responsibility for sales representatives in areas like reporting, complaint handling, refund and pricing.

Many other major organisations in UK have also started practising QWL improvement programmes for the general betterment of their organisation.

Sweden

The decision-making power in Sweden mostly lays with management as they have a right to 'hire and fire' and 'to distribute and manage jobs'. But with the increase in manpower problem,the managements are taking steps recently towards participative management. According to Ageavold, an academician, efforts were made in redesigning work and making workers participation effective.

Italy

Italy is a scene of high attention paid towards QWL in early 1970s, then decline in attention during later years of 1970s, as they perceived QWL as a 'peripheral problem'. And in recent years, the Government of Italy is again taking all steps to increase QWL consciousness among organisations with setting up of organisations like 'Kstitue de studi Lavora' and 'Istituto di Ricerca Intervento Svi Sistemi Organiativi'.

Organisations like 'Olivetti', 'Fiat', 'Proctor and Gamble', 'IBM', 'Italidev' and 'Philips' and practising QWL improvement programmes.

West Germany

West Germany like many other countries had become concerned about working conditions and other labour problems due to decreased productivity and industrial unrest.

As a measure towards improving quality of work life that Federal Ministry of Labour and Social Affairs introduced a research programme on humanisation of work in 1974. The concentration was on problems of industrial workers, particularly those from basic and metal processing industries. After 1976 the attention was on future orientation of the programmes and the priority was in the contents of such programmes.

Japan

Japan has always been first in introducing labour welfare programmes, maintaining sound labour management relations and practicing any new concept which ensure good industrial atmosphere. In case of QWL, Japan can be said as torch-bearer in introducing QWL—improvement programmes.

Their success in implementing QWL—improvement programmes can be mostly attributed to the positive attitudes of both management and employees and also extensive support from Government in all possible ways.

The Japanese have a two-way approach towards QWL—improvement programmes i.e., flexible employment of work force and employees general acceptance to technological changes.

Many other western and some of the Asian countries are also contributing towards QWL - improvement programmes.

India

India is a country with various cultures, value systems and varied interests. As such it is difficult to assess the impact of a particular concept in the country as a whole. For example, Lahiri and Srivastava (1976) had found out from their study in one of the industries that extrinsic rewards are more important to the workers, whereas Dayal and Sharma (1975) in another similar study carried out in still another industry concluded that intrinsic rewards are more important to the workers. In another study, Dayal says that Indian labour prefer paternalistic approach of management while Srivastava contradictorily says that workers would like to participate in decision-making given an opportunity, based on one of his studies.

Thorsrud[20], a researcher in this context, says "Even within the same country, there may be importances cultural differences with regard to the relative importance of motivating factors, and, therefore, there is a need to find local solutions to QWL problems, rather than applying uniform principles which cannot be adopted to local requirements".

As such, in India, the order of preference in improving various aspects of QWL should change from place to place, depending upon the preference of the workers and their attitudes at that place.

In fact, QWL improvement was not considered as important factor in India until recently. Because there were more impending factors like resource deficiency, environmental threats, serious financial problems and lack of consciousness among employees in this regard can also be considered as one of the reasons for delayed improvement of QWL. Though Trade Unions were playing an important role, their part is more of a destructive one. Their negative attitude towards management did not in any way help the improvement of QWL. In fact, workers selected for bipartite committees for decision-making are viewed by the Unions as their rivals.

There are also differences among the views of managements regarding QWL. Some have come to a stage, where they see human resource as a critical one in the developmental process and thus striving to take all steps to improve it, whereas the other organisations still did not realise the importance of Human Resources. Even if they realise, the improvement strategies confine themselves to increasing pay scales and introducing some welfare measures. They ignore the other aspect i.e., the higher order needs of the employees. This is so, especially in case of small and medium scale industries in backward states. Whereas large-scale industries and multi-nationals are fast realising the need for improvement of QWL.

The Government's intervention in this regard is minimum. The inclusion of the concept workers participation in Management did not in any way influence the improvement of QWL. The Ministry of Human Resource Development is taking active steps to implement some of the Human Resource Development programmes to which QWL correlates.

What is important in India at this stage is developing consciousness among all sections of industry i.e., workers, unions and management. Once these parties view QWL with a positive approach, the improvement programme can be effectively planned and implemented. Because a positive relationship between improved QWL and increase in worker's satisfaction is almost already established.

Measuring QWL

Various criterias are evolved in past two decades to measure quality of work life. Various researchers who carried on studies in this area came up with various criterias which are not entirely different from each other. As cited earlier, though many criterias evolved, Walton's eight factors are considered as a most comprehensive criteria for measurement of QWL. Let us proceed to critically examine Waltons eight-factor criteria.

The eight-point criteria of Walton to measure Quality of Work Life include :

(i) Adequate and fair compensation.

(ii) Safe, healthful working conditions.

(iii) Opportunity to develop human capacities.

(iv) Opportunity for career growth.

(v) Social integration in the work force.

(vi) Constitutionalism

(vii) Work and Quality of Life

(viii) Social relevance.

(i) Adequate and Fair Compensation :

In spite of the importance gained by the other factors during last two decades, compensation plays a greater role in employee's satisfaction. Especially in a country like India, where the employee welfare programmes take back seat, compensation is the main source of satisfaction of the employee.

Compensation package includes all other fringe benefits and social welfare programmes. Fringe benefits gives employee a feeling of gaining something extra. Recently, the concepts fringe benefits and social security measures are gaining importance in Indian industrial scene. Free transportation or transportation at minimum cost, hospital facility, group insurance programmes, retirement benefits are some of the important welfare programmes.

What is adequate and fair is another question for discussion. What is adequate at one place may not be same in the other. Organisations at rural, semi-urban regions can satisfy their employees with comparatively lower levels of compensation than their urban based counterparts. The urban based organisations usually compensate the extra cost of living, through higher Dearness Allowances, keeping basic the same.

Fair wages defined as " .... the wage which is above the minimum but below the living wage".[21] The levels of the fair wages also change depending upon cost of living. As the cost of living increases, the employees demand for more pay. Organisations fix pay ranges through different methods. They may fix wages comparing with other organisations in same region or similar organisation. They may fix taking cost of the living into account. They may also fix pay levels based upon their capacity to pay etc. But usually while fixing pay, all these factors are considered.

(ii) Safe and Healthy Working Conditions :

Physical working conditions is the second most important aspect in measuring QWL as Walton rightly categorised, Employees who spend a lot of time at their workplace consider the physical working conditions an important factor.

Especially chemical industries, engineering industries, fertilizer industries etc., where potential possibility of danger exists, the management has to take extra care to protect its employees. But most of such industries are covered by Factories Act which prescribes norms and conditions to be adopted in such industries to protect its employees.

But apart from above mentioned industries, others also have to take steps to maintain proper physical conditions. Proper seating arrangements, water facility, fresh air and good sanitary conditions are important to the employees who engage themselves in desk work. Absence of such good conditions may result in ailments like back pain and romantic pains which inturn frustrates the employees who may develop stress. Physical conditions at work places which is second home for employees is thus an important factor in measuring QWL.

(iii) Opportunity to Develop Human Capacities

An employee is most satisfied, given an opportunity to use

and develop his capabilities. According to Maslow, people want to satisfy their higher order needs once they satisfy their basic needs like fair pay and good physical condition. These higher order needs include recognition and social status.

More regulations and control mechanism by the management may dissatisfy the employee. This was the very reason why Taylor was criticised. An employee, provided optimum degree of freedom in work can improve himself on the job which gives him immense satisfaction. Periodic discussions with the employees, calling for his suggestions, and framing work groups like Quality Circles help employee in improving his capabilities on job. Proper training through various methods not only at the beginning but from time to time also helps an employee to improve his capabilities which in turn satisfy him.

(iv) Opportunity for Career Growth :

The employees seek career growth more and more recently. Job security ceased to satisfy employees. Employee tends to drift from a job which do not promise career growth. More and more organisations are helping employees in this direction by helping them draw their career paths. The organisations have a counsellor for this purpose, who helps the employees.

Not only drawing career paths, but the organisations also help employer achieve next position through training. Organisational chart is so prepared to accommodate employees in next higher position. Internal promotion system is gaining importance. The employee is prepared to take up a higher position where there is a possibility.

Prolonged employment in the same position may cause employee develop stress. Care is to be taken to chart proper career charts for employees at some level so as a balance of human resource in the organisation is maintained.

v) Social Integration in the Work Force :

According to Walton, a satisfying identify and self-esteem are influenced by five characteristics of the work place: freedom from prejudice, egalitarianism, upward mobility, supportive work groups and community of feelings, and interpersonal openness.[22]

Freedom from prejudice, egalitarianism and upward mobility are the steps to be necessary taken by the management.

Whereas supportive work groups and committees of feelings and interpersonal openness are the result of effort from both management and workers. Though the initiative is to be from management, the employees also should give their complete support and co-operation to make the efforts of management a success.

An organisation can possess supportive work groups and interpersonal openness. In other words, industrial democracy' through establishing 'work committees'- which intend to "promote measures for securing and preserving amity between employer and workmen and to that end to comment upon matter of their common interest or concern and endeavour to settle any material differences of opinion in respect of such matters".[23]

Another step in this direction could be setting up of Joint Management Councils'. These were first set up by Industrial Disputes Act 1847, in 1958. 'Joint Management Councils' were meant to (a) improve working conditions, productivity and communication; (b) assist in the administration of law and collective agreements; (c) encourage suggestions from workers and (d) create a sense of participation. [24]

Encouraging participative management schemes help in establishing industrial democracy in the organisation which in turn encourages social integartion in the organisation.

(iv) Constitutionalism :

Bias on part of management, lack of privacy, improper process of discipline etc., tamper the constitutionalism of an Organisation. The constitutionalism can be considered as hygiene factor i.e., though it may not satisfy or motivate the employees considerably. The absence of it is definitely felt by the employees and may have adverse effects.

Though employees consider work place their second home they may not want to disclose or discuss their private lives at work place. As such management should take steps to maintain its employees privacy unless, he himself come out with his problems, where the management can offer some counseling or any other help. So as in case of bias, it is most dissatisfying to an employee to find out that his colleague is being treated differently from him, which will have an adverse effect on his QWL.

(vii) Work and Quality of Life :

The very purpose of worker being at work place is his work. As such work itself is of great importance. Satisfactory work can influence the employee's QWL immensely. A challenging work which utilises the capabilities of employees plays important role in QWL. Right person for right job is the motto gaining importance.

Emery and Thorsurd (1969)[25] identified six psychological requirements of working people.

(a) The need for variety in the content of a job.

(b) The need for being able to learn on the job and go on learning.

(c) The need for some minimal area of decision-making that the individual can call his own.

(d) The need for some minimal degree of social support and recognition in the work place.

(e) The need for the individual to be able to relate what he does and what he produces to his social life.

(f) The need to feel that the job leads to some sort of desirable future.

(viii) Social Relevance of Work :

The employees feel a need to relate their work socially. For example, those in service-oriented organisations who directly relate their jobs socially and can gain immediate recognition in a group are most satisfied. If his organisation is attracted/criticised by the Government or public on any aspect, the employee develops stress and is frustrated.

As such social relevance of the work of each employee is very important in measuring his QWL.

Specific Issues of QWL

While the management and unions claim any improvement in facilities and financial benefits, the Personnel Managers task is to identify other specific issues of QWL pertaining in his own organisation and work on them. The American authors Klatt, Mudrick and Schuster and identified 11 specific issues in general which we can also adopt.[26] They are :

1. Pay and Stability of Employment

Pay without stability of employment cannot satisfy the employee. Though stability of employment is not a serious problem in India, the management should ensure its employees stability to make them part of the organisation in its real sense.

2. Occupational Stress

Stress is a condition of strain on one's emotions, though process and physical condition.[27] Preferring all types of jobs inevitably causes stress, though the intensity may vary from job to job. As such job performance depends upon effective management of stress in addition to the other factors which in turn depends upon identification of sources of stress.[28]

3. Organisational Health Programmes

The idea behind such health centres is to develop mental health by maintaining good physical health. This can be done through encouraging employee take up physical exercises, games and sports.

4. Alternative Work Schedule

Each employee may have his own preferences of working hours. The management can introduce schemes like work at home, flexible working hours, staggered hours, reduced work week and part-time employment.

5. Participative Management and Control of Work

As discussed earlier, participative management is life blood to QWL which creates a feeling of commitment among the workers, thus improving their QWL.

6. Recognition

Appreciate an employee in public and criticise him in private. Recognition and appreciation is a magic work which changes anyone's attitudes towards anyone. Recognition at an appropriate time can improve personal relations in the organisation.

7. Superior-Subordinate Relations

Relations between boss and subordinate is an important aspect in improving total work culture, productivity and QWL of any organisation.

8. Grivance Procedure

Grievance procedure is to be handled carefully, because between the two parties, one is bound to dissatisfy. The management using apathy and concern should try to reduce this dissatisfaction as much as possible.

9. Adequacy of Resources

Adequate resources should be ensured to the employees on work. Inadequacy of resources may cause stress to employees who are prepared to work but cannot find resources.

10. Seniority and Merit in Promotion and Employment

Either seniority or merits are usually considered for promotions and employment. Management has to consider either one depending upon the attitudes of employees. Sometimes they can also consider both.

11. Employment on Permanent Basis

Stable employment is something which gives confidence to the employee which is prime factor for good employment. With given job security, the employee strive for the organisation.

Barriers to QWL

Though the positive effect of Quality of Work Life is already established, all parties of the organisation still resist to any schemes or procedure to improve QWL. The management may feel that the QWL at present level is satisfactory enough and no steps need be taken to improve it. They fail to measure the impact of improved QWL on the psyche of the employee, though all employees basically aspire for satisfaction of employees.

Employees on the other hand resist to changes as discussed earlier, with a pre-conceived notion that any scheme, the management takes up would be to increase production without extra cost.

Another barrier to the improvement of QWL is lack of financial resources. The employer with his limited financial resources think twice before providing better working conditions, offering better wage and implementing other programmes of QWL.

However, the situation is slowly changing for good. All parties of organisation, i.e., employer, employees and unions are realising the importance of QWL. Employees also are taking up awareness programmes to educate employees in this regard and then implement QWL improvement programmes.

Strategies for improving Quality of Work Life, according to Subba Rao, are self-managed work teams, job redesign and enrichment, effective leadership and supervisory behaviour, career development alternative work schedules, job security.[29] All the above steps depict the importance of management's efforts in this regard. By implementing such changes, the management can create sense of involvement, commitment, and togetherness among the employees which paves way for better quality of work life.

Not only human resources managements aspects but QWL consists of whole parcel of terms and notions.

- Industrial effectiveness
- Human Resource Development
- Organisational effectiveness
- Work restructure
- Job enrichment
- Socio-technical systems
- Working humanisation
- Group work concept
- Labour management co-operation

As such QWL enters into all major parts of HRM. Its significance is to be duly identified and should be given importance.

Notes :

1. Arthur Lewis, "The History of Economic Growth", George Allen & Urwin Ltd., London, 1965, p. ii.
2. Terry L. Leap, Michael D. Crino, Personnel/Human Resource Management, Macmillan International Ltd., p. 18.
3. McGregor, Douglas, 'The Human Side of Enterprise', Tata McGraw-Hill Publishing Co. Ltd., New Delhi, 1960, p. 4.
4. P.F. Drucker, The Practice of Management, Allied, New Delhi, 1970, p. 12.
5. P. Subba Rao, & V.S.P. Rao, Personnel/Human Resource Management, Konark Publishers Pvt. Ltd., pp. 1–2.

6. Sheldon Oliver, 'Philosophy of Management', Prentice Hall, Englwood Cliffs, 1923, p. 27.
7. Edwin B. Flippo, 'Principles of Personnel Management', McGraw-Hill Kogakusha Ltd., Tokyo, 76, p. 8.
8. Wendell L. French 'The Personnel Management', Houghton Mifflin Company, Boston, 1978, p. 3.
9. Mahaveer Jain "A Study of some psychological indicators of QWL", unpublished thesis, University of Delhi, 1986, p. 1.
10. Rosow, J.M., 'Quality of Working Life and Productivity' The Double Pay Off, a paper presented at Conference held at America Institute Inc., Chicago, Illiois, April, 1977.
11. Walton R.E., 'Criteria for quality of working life' in Davis L., et. al., The Free Press, London, 1977, pp. 91–112.
12. AT & T', QWL Expriment—A Practical Case Study, Management Review Summer, 1983, pp. 12–16.
13. Guest R.H. 'Quality of Work Life—Learning from Terry-town', Harward Business Review, July–August, 1979, pp. 28–39.
14. Nadler, D.A. and Lawler E.E., 'Quality of Work Life, Perspective and Direction', Organisational Dynamics, Winter 1983, Vol. 11 (3), pp. 20–30.
15. De, N.R., 'Some Dimensions of Quality of Working Life', paper presented at the National Seminar on Quality of Working Life, Bombay, 1976, pp. 22–27.
16. Keith Davis, 'Human Behaviour at Work : Tata McGraw Hill Publishing Company Ltd., New Delhi, 1981. p. 273.
17. P. Subba Rao & V.S.P. Rao, op. cit., pp. 52–53.
18. Cherns, A., 'Using the Social Sciences', London : Rovlledge and Vegan Paul, 1979.
19. Emery, F.E., and Thorsurd, E., 'Form and Content in Industrial Democracy' Tavistock, London, 1969.
20. Thorsrud, 'QWL in the First and the Third World' Productivity, Vol. 22 (4), 1982. pp. 3–11.
21. P. Subba Rao & V.S.P. Rao, op. cit., p. 47.
22. Klatt, Murduck and Schuster, Human Resource Management, Chartex E. Merrill Publishing Company, Ohio, 1985, p. 584.
23. Baldev R. Sharma, 'Industrial Democracy : The Indian Experience Indian Journal of Industrial Relations. Vol. 22, No. 3, Jan. 1987, p. 256.

24. Ibid. pp. 256–257.

25. Emery, F.E., and Thorsurd, E., "Form and Content in Industrial Democracy", Tavistocks, London, 1969.

26. Klatt, Murdick and Schuster, op. cit., pp. 585–592.

27. Keith Davis, 'Human Behaviour at Work' Tata McGraw Hill Publishing Company, Ltd., 1981, New Delhi. p. 273.

28. P. Subba Rao and Anitha, 'Stress Management' in V.S.P. Rao and Srilatha, 'Organisation Stress' Discovery Publishing House, New Delhi, 1991, p. 263.

29. P. Subba Rao & V.S.P. Rao, op. cit., p. 203.

2

Evolution and Growth of Andhra Bank and The Vysya Bank Ltd.

Banking Industry is a very important tool in the construction of economic structure of any country. What was started as simple economic intermediare, has become all pervasive, covering all areas of business. Any business, whatever may be the nature, has to transact with bank at sometime or the other.

Banks provide wide range of financial services, Banking made it possible for businessman to transact with their counter-parts on entire globe. The financial transactions have shifted from transactions in coins to introduction of credit cards and micro chips. Financial transactions of business have become so simple and manageable that businessmen can leave this part entirely to banks and concentrate on other important aspects.

In a developing country like India, banks also have social responsibilities like uplifting the weaker sections and financing the social projects. Banking industry in India has been playing a pivotal role in rebuilding the Indian economy by extending its network to the backward and rural areas, financing agriculture, small industries, weaker sections of the society etc., in addition to providing finance to industry and business.

The evaluation and growth of banking industry can be re-viewed in two stages i.e.,

1. Pre-Nationalisation (prior to 1969)
2. Post-Nationalisation (1969 onwards).

Though Banking industry has its roots ever since 1688, in India it is only after 1939 that the industry has achieved subsistence after initial setbacks and failures. There were many small banks mushrooming until 1936 with a very high rate of failures.

An important phenomena during this period is that individual banks have come up in place of indigenous bankers. Table 2.1 depicts the number of banks, their internal resources, deposits and advances during 1942 to 1948. The table shows an increase in the number of banks from 44 scheduled banks and 431 non-scheduled banks to 77 scheduled and 541 non-scheduled banks during 1948. The table also shows a steady and continuous increase in capital, deposits and advances of scheduled banks. The growth was not continuous and somewhat impaired during later years of the period in case of non-scheduled banks. This phenomena can be attributed mainly to the policy of Reserve Bank of India (RBI) to encourage scheduled banks and partly due to partition of country during 1947 and the disturbances that followed.

The Government of India felt a need for central bank of the country to regulate the banking system in the country which took the form of RBI. It was declared as Central Bank of India under Reserve Bank of India Act, 1934.

Multiple amalgamations and liquidations have taken place during this period. Initially 11 banks went into voluntary liquidations and 4 scheduled banks in Bengal were amalgamated with United Bank of India Ltd. The process of liquidations and amalgamations were very rapid even after 1950s especially in case of non-scheduled banks. As such there was a rapid decline in the number of both scheduled and non-scheduled banks. The number of scheduled banks came down from 75 in 1951 to 57 in 1969. The number of non-scheduled banks had come down from 469 to 14 during this period. A detailed picture of these particulars is presented in Table 2.2.

With a goal of achieving social ends that nationalisation could secure without taking over banks into public ownership, the then Government imposed social control over the banks on 14th December 1967. Making a statement in Lok Sabha, Deputy Prime

Table 2.1 : Banking Industry in India during 1939–48 *(Rs in lakhs)*

Item	1939	%	1940	%	1941	%	1942	%	1943	%	1944	%	1945	%	1946	%	1947	%	1948	%
1. No. of Banks :																				
a) Imperial Banks	1	–	1	–	1	–	1	–	1	–	1	–	1	–	1	–	1	–	1	–
b) Scheduled Banks	39	–	41	–	44	–	44	–	57	–	69	–	75	–	79	–	80	–	77	–
c) Non-sch. Banks	643	–	592	–	415	–	431	–	489	–	559	–	646	–	543	–	544	–	541	–
Total	**683**	–	**634**	–	**460**	–	**476**	–	**547**	–	**629**	–	**722**	–	**623**	–	**625**	–	**619**	–
2. Paid-up Capital :																				
a) Imperial Banks	1123	39	1125	38	1125	36	1138	33	1148	27	1163	22	1170	19	1186	17	1186	27	1190	16
b) Scheduled Banks	1194	42	1267	42	1360	44	1625	48	2372	56	3206	60	3877	62	4331	65	4617	66	5004	67
c) Non-sch. Banks	548	19	587	20	631	20	667	19	525	17	939	18	1211	19	1182	18	1209	17	1261	17
Total	**2865**	**100**	**2979**	**100**	**3116**	**100**	**3430**	**100**	**4045**	**100**	**5308**	**100**	**6258**	**100**	**6699**	**100**	**7102**	**100**	**7455**	**100**
3. Deposits :																				
a) Imperial Banks	8784	43	9603	42	10892	42	16346	42	21453	37	23778	32	25937	28	27167	27	28659	29	28029	29
b) Scheduled Banks	9374	46	10610	47	12904	49	18934	49	32450	55	45657	58	54280	60	61121	62	61987	63	59383	63
c) Non-Sch. Banks	2187	11	2450	11	2494	09	3471	09	4803	08	7560	10	11075	12	10403	11	8332	08	7655	08
Total	**20345**	**100**	**22663**	**100**	**26290**	**100**	**38751**	**100**	**58706**	**100**	**76995**	**100**	**98691**	**100**	**95067**	**100**	**98978**	**100**	**97567**	**100**
4. Loans and advances :																				
a) Imperial Banks	4828	40	3231	32	3888	32	3379	29	4060	23	7023	26	7297	21	9427	21	8915	21	9600	23
b) Scheduled Banks	5258	44	4895	49	6276	52	6067	52	10893	61	15788	59	22155	63	30467	67	28413	66	27292	64
c) Non-Sch. Banks	1964	16	1854	19	1850	16	2165	19	2778	16	3976	15	5732	16	5871	12	5537	13	5286	13
Total	**12050**	**100**	**9980**	**100**	**12014**	**100**	**11601**	**100**	**17731**	**100**	**26767**	**100**	**35184**	**100**	**45765**	**100**	**42865**	**100**	**42178**	**100**
5. Investments :																				
a) Imperial Banks	3802	48	4857	50	6439	50	11641	51	13020	42	14863	38	15418	33	15453	34	16419	35	16125	35
b) Scheduled Banks	3651	46	4245	44	5852	45	10177	45	16702	54	13208	58	27902	60	27019	59	18485	60	27953	60
c) Non-Sch. Banks	523	06	552	06	652	05	918	04	1123	04	1808	04	3199	07	3416	07	2631	05	2455	05
Total	**7976**	**100**	**9654**	**100**	**12943**	**100**	**22736**	**100**	**30845**	**100**	**29879**	**100**	**46519**	**100**	**45888**	**100**	**37535**	**100**	**46533**	**100**

Source : Compiled from various issues of Statistical Tables relating to banks in India, Published by Reserve Bank of India.

Table 2.2 : Banking Industry in India during 1951–69

(Rs in lakhs)

Item	*1951*	*%*	*1956*	*%*	*1961*	*%*	*1968*	*%*	*1967*	*%*	*1968*	*%*	*1969*	*%*
1. No. of Banks :														
a) State Bank of India	1	–	1	–	1	–	1	–	1	–	1	–	1	–
b) Scheduled Banks	75	–	71	–	66	–	59	–	57	–	56	–	57	–
c) Non-sch. Banks	469	–	333	–	210	–	27	–	20	–	16	–	14	–
Total	**545**	**–**	**405**	**–**	**277**	**–**	**87**	**–**	**78**	**–**	**73**	**–**	**72**	**–**
2. Paid-up Capital and Reserves :														
a) State Bank of India	1198	16	1201	17	1383	18	1695	17	1785	17	1887	18	1998	18
b) Scheduled Banks	4880	66	4814	66	5672	74	7984	81	8284	81	8510	81	8983	81
c) Non-sch. Banks	1337	18	1208	17	580	08	213	02	202	02	174	01	160	01
Total	**7415**	**100**	**7223**	**100**	**7635**	**100**	**9892**	**100**	**10271**	**100**	**10571**	**100**	**11141**	**100**
3. Deposits :														
a) State Bank of India	23091	28	23547	23	53246	29	78610	23	85840	23	94983	22	111411	23
b) Scheduled Banks	51734	63	72536	70	125995	69	255899	76	282360	76	323427	77	369374	76
c) Non-sch. Banks	6977	09	7375	07	3996	02	2460	01	2658	01	2721	01	2439	01
Total	**81802**	**100**	**103458**	**100**	**183237**	**100**	**336969**	**100**	**370858**	**100**	**421131**	**100**	**483224**	**100**
4. Loans and advances :														
a) State Bank of India	14246	29	14016	21	25531	23	54068	24	59550	24	75522	26	84136	25
b) Scheduled Banks	30192	61	47829	72	83586	75	170731	75	189639	76	210977	73	255462	75
c) Non-sch. Banks	4742	10	4254	07	2506	02	1373	01	1286	–	1311	01	1233	–
Total	**49180**	**100**	**66099**	**100**	**111623**	**100**	**226172**	**100**	**250475**	**100**	**287810**	**100**	**340831**	**100**
5. Investments :														
a) State Bank of India	8516	26	10687	26	23673	36	29870	28	31075	27	33245	26	35816	25
b) Scheduled Banks	21727	66	27043	66	40264	62	77605	72	81772	72	95746	73	108808	75
c) Non-sch. Banks	2658	08	3195	08	1419	02	887	–	1172	01	1186	01	988	–
Total	**32901**	**100**	**40925**	**100**	**65356**	**100**	**108362**	**100**	**114019**	**100**	**130177**	**100**	**145612**	**100**

Source : Compiled from various issues of Statistical Tables relating to banks in India, Published by Reserve Bank of India

Minister of the day, Morarji Desai listed out objectives of social control as, prevention of monopolistic trends, concentration of economic power, misdirection of resources and to make banking system serve our socio-economic objectives.

Two steps were mainly taken in the direction. One was setting up of National Credit Council on December 22, 1967 to assess periodically the available resources of credit and ensure its equitable and purposeful distribution among several sectors by keeping national economic development in view. It is also council's duty to assess the demand for banks credit, determine priority for granting loans, coordinate the lending and investment policies of commercial and cooperative banks.

The second step in this direction was the enactment of Banking Laws (Amendment) Act of 1968. The amended act provided for a change in board of directors from industrialists to non-industrialists, agriculturists, economists, accountants, lawyers etc.

Through social controls the Government expected banks to extend their credit facilities to priority sectors like agriculture, small industry, transport operation, small trade and business, students persuing higher studies in India and abroad.

For this purpose, the priority sectors consist of (i) Agriculture, (ii) Small-Scale Industries, (iii) Small traders, (iv) Small Business enterprises, (v) Professionals & self-employed, (vi) Transport operators and (vii) Education.

Nationalisation of Banks

Social control had proved to be of little or no use to the priority sectors. Soon after Government imposing social controls, the bankers found out excuses to avoid credit to priority sectors. This is quite evident from the fact that during three annual plans two per cent of credit was provided for agriculture.

The Government in these circumstances was forced to take extreme step i.e., nationalisation of commercial banks. As first step, the Government nationalised 14 major commercial banks with deposits of more than Rs. 50 crores on July 19, 1969.

Nationalisation of banks was mainly targeted towards an overall economic development which could not be achieved through commercial banks. Government nationalised six more commercial banks in 1980.

The main objective of nationalisation of banks in India were as follows:

(i) Removing control over banks by a few;

(ii) Providing adequate training and reasonable terms of service for bank employees.

(iii) To extend banking facilities in unbanked and underbanked centres especially in rural areas.

(iv) To ensure an increased flow of assistance to the sectors neglected hitherto, and

(v) To encourage the new progressive classes of entrepreneurs etc.

Post-Nationalisation Development of Banking Industry (1969–92)

The development of Banking industry after nationalisation is presented in the Table 2.3. TheTable clearly shows an increase in branches from 6,596 in 1969 to 41,996 in 1992. Especially the rural branches registered a record increase in the number of branches with a percentage as high as 92.67. These figure evidently show how the Government has been concentrating on development of

Table 2.3 : Progress of Nationalised Banks during 1969–1992

Item	June 1969	June 1992
1. Total no. of offices in India	6596	41996
2. Rural	1505	20535
Semi-urban	2622	9124
Urban	1176	6863
Metropolitan	1293	5474
3. Population per office	65000	11000
4. Deposits (Rs. in Crores)	3897	235922
5. Advances (Rs. in Crores)	3035	143648
6. Priority Sector Advances (Rs. in crores)	441	44995

Source : RBI Bulletin. January, 1993, supplement : Report on Trend and Progress of Banking in India.

rural areas. The advances extended to priority sectors increased from a meagre Rs. 441 crores to Rs. 44,995 crores.

Priority Sectors

The very purpose of bank's nationalisation was to serve priority sectors which failed to get any attention or care from commercial banks before 1969. Introduction of social controls did not prove to be of much use. The definition of priority sectors kept changing. In 1969, priority sectors included of agriculture, small industry and exports.[1] But in due course of time, the term priority sectors kept expanding. New areas of priority were identified from time to time. According to the report of RBI on trend and progress of banking in India, priority sectors apart from agriculture, small business and exports, include setting up of industrial estates, road and water, transport operators, retail trade, small business, professionals and self-employed persons, education, housing of weaker sections etc.[2]

Table 2.4 shows the number of accounts, and average advances to prior sectors during 1969 to 1992. While advances to all priority sectors shows a clear increase, agriculture alone draws about 41% of the total advances extended to priority sectors. In spite of many areas being categorised, under priority sector, agriculture still holds its importance.

Table 2.4 : Achievement of Targets/Sub-targets in respect of Public Sector Banks as on March, 1992

(Rs. in Crores)

	Item	March 1992
1.	Net Bank Credit	114502
2.	Priority Sector Advances percentage to Net Bank Credit	44995 (40.00)
3.	Direct Advances to Agriculture percentage to Net Bank Credit	17020 (14.90)
4.	Advances to Weaker Sections percentage to Net Bank Credit	10948 (09.60)
5.	Advances under D.R.I. Scheme percentage to outstanding advances at the end of December, 1992	727 (0.70)

Source : RBI Bulletin. January, 1993, supplement : Report on Trend and Progress of Banking in India.

While the total advances to priority sectors increase from Rs. 4.41 crores to Rs. 44,995 crores, average advance per account reduced from Rs. 16,962 to Rs. 12,639. Other sectors include road and water transport operators, professionals and self-employed and for education. Housing loan to weaker sections and consumption loans etc., for which advances increased from Rs. 22 crores to Rs. 8,842 crores.

Branch Expansion

Importance was given to opening up of new branches in rural and semi-urban areas. Most of these branches were opened in backward areas, and rural areas. The growth of branch expansion during the period of July 1969 and June 1979 was more than that of the expansion of branches since inception of banking industry in India. Table 2.5 gives a clear picture of growth of branch expansion and the percentage of new bank branches in rural areas between 1975 and 1979.

Table 2.5 : Branch Expansion of Commercial Banks (1969–1979)

Year	*Total Offices opened*	*Offices opened at hither to unbanked areas*
1975	2337	739 (31.60)
1976	3191	1324 (41.50)
1978–79 (July-June)	2190	1478 (67.00)
1969–79 (July–June)	21881	11476 (52.00)

Note : Figures in Paranthes are percentage to total offices
Source : Compiled from RBI Reports.

Between 1950 and 1969, the total number of bank offices that were opened was 4,230. Between July 1969 and June 1979, bank offices were 21,881. The average population covered by rural branches was 65,000 at the time of nationalisation, which was reduced to 7,000 by the end of June 1986. As such opening up of new branches was clearly in favour of rural areas.

Deposit Mobilisation

Nationalisation of the banks had inspired confidence in customers which in turn attracted more deposits. Branch expansion also considerably helped in this way. The introduction of deposit insurance scheme was also another important factor for the increase in the deposits with banks.

From June 1969, the deposits with banks had increased from Rs. 3,873 crores to Rs. 7,570 crores in June 1973. Similar increase was recorded during June 1973 and June 1976.

Genesis and Growth of Andhra Bank

Incorporation of Andhra Bank

During the days of struggle for independence, freedom fighters from Andhra province who were in the vanguard like Pattabhi Seetharmaih, thought of fighting for separate Andhra State. As a part of the struggle they came up with many regional institutions like Andhra Saleeya Kalasala at Machilipatnam, a cottage industries wing and a chemical engineering section in 1910. Krishna Co-operative bank was started in 1915. Andhra Provincial Co-operative Conference was convened in 1918 at Rajahmundry. Also the call of Father of Nation stressing the need for National institutions initiated freedom fighters of Andhra province think of establishing various institutions. In the own words of Andhra Bank -"The clavison call of Father of Nation, Mahatma Gandhi in the second and third decades of this century bestirred the Indian Nation from its slumber of centuries. Patriotic fervour and impatience gripped the country. The urge to establish and nurture the national Institutions to serve national needs and to impart meaning and content to political freedom; when in fact came, was characteristic of those years".[3]

In these circumstances Dr. Pattabhi Seetharmaiah initiated an idea of starting a credit institution to cater to the needs of the people of Andhra province which would be managed by Andhras. Thus Andhra Bank was established at Machilipatnam, on November 20, 1923 which actually started functioning from November 28, 1923.

The administration and management of the bank did not prove to be a cakewalk for the incorporators though the bank was established with good ideals and with an objective "to pool the economic resources of the country and the Andhra in particular and to cater to the needs of mercantile community, provide short-term credit to agriculturists and give a helping hand to the industry by providing for its working funds".[4]

The problems started with inculcating the habit of banking as banking was not a habit of the people of Andhra.

Though capital mobilisation was made possible by efforts of the incorporators, appointing directors has proved to be a major problem, with the agents of Imperial Bank convassing among general public, not to associate with New Bank. As such general public also hesitated to become shareholders. The problem of appointment of Managing Directors was solved by the appointment of Pattabhi Seetharamaiah by whose sincere efforts, the bank had come into existence.

The Imperical Bank of India already made its stand clear by convassing against Andhra Bank among general public of Andhra. As such Andhra Bank faced a peculiar problem that no trader or business came forward to claim for loans contrary to the situation now where there is always competition in obtaining loans. As such the business of the newly started bank was hampered.

During Great Depression in 1930's confusion prevailed among money markets all over the world which was also experienced by Andhra bank.

As the banks were just recovering from the effect of Great Depression, two South Indian banks - Travancore National and Quilon Bank Ltd., collapsed completely during 1938, which had raised doubts about banking system itself among general public. The habit of depositing in bank and obtaining loans which was just catching up had suffered severe setback. Doubts were regarding the very existence and future of banking system in South India. The Reserve Bank of India which was described as banker's bank and lender of last resort could not help in anyway. It was a very long period before normally resorted into the bank.

As Andhra Bank was still in the process of recovery from the bad image through failure of two South Indian Banks, the war broke out. India was also involved in war, and all major parts had become strategic points. It was the Japanese air raids on Visakhapatnam and Kakinada that caused a lot of fear among the people of that place. Their lives were at stake - not talking about saving anything for future. As such the deposits of the bank touched rock bottom.

As a consequence of war expenditure the notes circulation was increased which resulted in unexpected inflation. The businessmen and industrialists were enjoying unlimited profits which they turned over to start new industrial ventures and apart from that some of them ventured into banking industry itself. With ample of resources being available these newly started banks soon started to expand their operations through expansions causing severe competition to the small banks which are established on purely regional basis like Andhra Bank. Andhra Bank had to lose fair position of their deposits and some of very important profitable ventures owing to the competition.

Growth of Andhra Bank

The Andhra Bank moved its head office in 1963 from Machilipatnam to Hyderabad, capital of Andhra Pradesh for administrative conveniences. Bharat Lakshmi Bank, also started by Pattabhi Seetharmaiah, merged with Andhra Bank in 1964. The Government of India during its second round of nationalisation, nationalised Andhra Bank on April 15, 1980.

Andhra Bank was the first bank to introduce credit card system in India. The "custodian of Andhra Bank is appointed as the member of Regional Board of Directors for Visa International for Asia and Pacific in September 1981.

Andhra Bank growth in physical and economic terms can be critically examined through some of the following aspects :

1. Capital Structure,
2. Branch expansion,
3. Structural changes in the organisation; and
4. Lead bank

1. Capital Structure

The Andhra bank was started with paid-up capital of Rs. 1,00,000/- initially when it was first incorporated in 1923. It maintained good balance between paid-up capital and deposits. Later in 1947, the capital rose to Rs. 25,00,000/- and continued with the same till 1954 until the capital crossed the mark of 30 lakhs. Later it was steadily growing till 1974 when the capital reached Rs. 50,40,700/-. Then in 1975 the capital was Rs. 1,00,00,000 which was continued till 1983. It increased to Rs. 22 crores in 1989-90. It is observed from the Table (2.6) that Andhra Bank has reserves and surplus to the tune of Rs. 40 crores, deposits Rs. 3225.70

Table 2.6 : The Capital Structure of Andhra Bank during 1987–1989–90

(Rs. in Crores)

Particulars	1987	1988-89	1989-90
Capital	17.00	22.00	22.00
Reserve fund and other reserves	26.35	34.00	40.00
From banks	3.28	23.80	21.86
From others	57.51	34.60	158.63
Total Advances	2080.63	2612.47	3067.02
Deposits	2138.14	2647.07	3225.70

Source : Economic & Planning Department, Andhra Bank, Hyderabad.

crores.

2) Branch Expansion

Branch expansion programme, a must for economic development was vigorously pursued by Indian banks to help them accelerate their deposits. Especially in a country like India, where general public are scattered from remote rural areas to metropolitan cities and where the mobilisation of public for the purpose of banking is very less, the banking inevitably has to go to public at their places, than they coming to urban areas for banking purpose. The Government of India was also encouraging branch expansion especially in rural areas with a purpose of promoting habit of banking among people. Stepping stone towards this branch expansion of Andhra Bank was starting first branch in Kakinada in 1929. Then, with the success of Kakinada branch, the expansion steadily grew at a slower pace initially and then rapidly. By 1951, 50 branches of Andhra Bank was operating. Number of branches operating raised to 155 by 1969. During this period, satellite offices and extension counters and pay offices were introduced, which helped in even rapid growth of branches. By 1984, total number of branches were 894 among which 789 were full-fledged.

Table 2.7 shows the growth of branches of Andhra Bank during 1985 to 1989-90. It is clear from the table that Andhra Bank opened its branches in rural, semi-urban, urban and metropolitan areas. The total number of branches increased to 931 in 1985 to 1055 in 1989-90.

Table 2.7 : Branch Expansion of Andhra Bank during 1985 to 1989-90

Branches	*1985*	*1986*	*1987*	*1988-89*	*1989-90*
Rural	352	352	387	395	427
Semi-urban	210	210	212	239	241
Urban	164	164	166	171	175
Metropolitan	99	100	100	101	102
Total	825	826	865	906	945
Clusters	84	84	83	80	76
Extension counters	21	23	27	31	37
Grand Total	**930**	**933**	**975**	**1017**	**1058**

Source : Personnel records, Head Office, Andhra Bank.

3) Staff

The staff of Andhra Bank are divided into three categories viz., officers, clerical staff, sub-ordinate Staff. Among officers, there are four grades viz., Selection Grade, Grade I, Grade II and Grade III.

Rapid branch expansion necessitated employment of more staff. It is surprising to know that the bank operated with just 3 members of staff initially. By 1953, the number of staff was 673. By 1959, the number increased to 1,083. Later by 1968, the staff on pay roll was 2,157, which was 3,216 in 1975. By 1982 the number crossed 10,000 mark and in 1984 the staff was 12,141. Growth of staff during 1989 to 1991 is presented in Table 2.8. It is observed from this table that the total staff increased from 14,772 to 15,064 during the period.

4) Lead Bank

Under the Lead Bank Scheme which was introduced in 1969, each district is entrusted to one bank. That particular bank has to survey the potential in the district, choose appropriate unit and impart technical knowledge.

Table 2.8 : Growth of Staff in Andhra Bank during 1987 to 1991

Year	*Officers*	*Clerks*	*Sub-staff*	*Total*
1987	5,178	7,058	2,536	14,772
1989 (March)	5,168	7,555	2,555	15,278
1990	5,117	7,858	2,629	15,604
1991	5,799	7,561	2,644	16,004

Source : Personnel records, Head Office, Andhra Bank.

Andhra Bank was made lead bank for five districts in the country viz., Guntur, West Godavari, East Godavari, Srikakulam and Ganjam. The performance of the bank in this respect was very satisfactory. The Bank achieved 147 per cent of the target in 1984.

Andhra Bank also sponsored two Regional Banks - Rishikulya Grameena Bank in Ganjam district of Orissa and Chaitanya Grameena Bank in Guntur district with the assistance of Andhra Bank in training and recruitment of personnel of in re-financing, both these banks are a success.

Andhra Bank is one of the oldest banks established in Andhra Pradesh initially to cater to the needs of people of Andhra Pradesh. But later, it expanded its branches to the other areas of the country. However, Andhra Bank plays a very important role in the banking habits of the people of Andhra Pradesh. In some rural areas the name Andhra Bank is synonymous to Bank. Whenever people need any banking facility like credit facility or for savings, they look up at Andhra Bank. The position reached by Andhra Bank today is longway from what it was with one branch and three staff members when it was first established in 1923.

Profile of Vysya Bank

Genesis and Growth of the Vysya Bank Ltd.

The Vysya Bank which made its humble beginning in 1930 is the largest private sector bank. It was started by some visionaries and philanthropists headed by late Margapuram Chengaiah, Chetty, the founder Chairman who was also known for his business acumen and encouragement to small traders. The bank was started in a small way at 489, Avenue Road Bangalore, which still remains as its Avenue Road Branch, to assist its large clients. The earnest effort put in the beginning was continued by a host of people like Pamidi Subbarama Chetty, S.V. Sreenivasa Setty, Yadalam, S. Gopala Krishna Setty, M.R. Arya, M.V.N. Setty, T.K.K. Bhagavat, Ramesh Gelli, and Presently by I. Sadasiva Gupta.

The bank had a slow but steady growth in the early years. By 1960 it had 19 branches and at the time of nationalisation of other banks it had 39 branches with deposits of Rs. 8.29 crores.

The post-nationalisation period saw lot of expansion an growth in the banking industry. It was in the years between 1971 and 1980 that Vysya Bank went through a phenomenal expansion both in terms of size and resources. Between 1974 and 1978 the branches grew from 72 to 185 and the deposits increased from Rs. 20 crores to Rs. 87.75 crores.[5] However, the bank had problems which hampered the rapid growth and it was between 1975 and 1985 that the bank was able to build its internal strength and had a very impressive growth rate. In 1984 and 1985, the bank slowly surged from its position as number four among private sector banks to the third position and from there to the first position which it seems determined to maintain.

Before the introduction of social control of banks, the affairs relating to the organisation was looked after mainly by Jayanthi Suryanarayana Chetty who had been associated with the bank for several years as its General Manager. He was the architect of the Bank's policies and procedures.

Vysya Bank is the largest in private sector in the country with over 289 branches spread over 11 states and two Union Territories having deposits and advances over Rs. 851 crores and Rs. 458 crores respectively, employing over 4983 persons, transacting all types of banking business and offering a wide spectrum of international banking facilities backed by a global network of correspondents.[6]

The Bank got the status of Scheduled Bank in 1948. With a view to imparting systematic training to its personnel, the bank started a training school in 1968. The school was upgraded into a college in 1976. A second unit of the college was opened in Hyderabad in March, 1984. In 1987, the Bank instituted its full-fledged integrated training college complex at Bangalore with modern amenities, teaching aids, hostel, air-conditioned conference hall facilities etc. Besides offering training to more than 2000 participants every year, the college functions as a research centre of the bank.

A quarterly house magazine captioned "Pragathi" was introduced by the Bank in 1978 with a view of providing a vehicle of communication of the employees of the Bank.

Social Welfare by Bank

In addition to orienting towards society's credit and economic needs, Vysya Bank has been constantly serving the social cause of the society by organising blood donation camps, medical checkup camps, eye care camps, hospital visits along with mobilising help to drought-stricken, flood-affected etc.[7] These welfare activities towards the society have brought in the institution and its employees a more humane and cordial approach resulting in the bank coming closer to people beyond the realms of routine banking.

Growth over the Decades

It is observed from reports that the Bank had seen its peak growth and performance in the last one decade. In fact, the growth in special thrust areas like profits, export credit etc.; have seen a three figure growth percentages. Nineteen Eighty could be termed a golden era with spectacular growth giving the Bank a position of distinction.

In many vital areas the bank's performance was relatively laudable. The bank crossed 40 per cent lending to the priority sectors stipulated by the RBI by the March 31, 1985, and it reached 42.5 per cent by December 1985. The year 1986 was indeed a historic one for Vysya Bank. The most significant aspect was that it attained the first position among the private banks excluding J & K Bank Limited which has certain in-built advantages and therefore cannot be compared with the rest of the scheduled commercial banks. The Bank's name topped the list among the private banks when its deposits crossed Rs. 400 crore mark by the end of 1985, recording a good growth rate.

Not being content with the internal business, they did well in the international business too. The bank has fully equipped International division to carry out the business on modern lines.

Vysya Bank is the only private bank in the country to have become a member of the Society for world wide Inter Financial Tele Communication (SWIFT) which will help to enhance speed in International transactions.

It is not just the growth in numbers that has put the bank in the premier pedestal, more than numbers, it has been its initiatives towards customer service, its fulfillment of obligations to society beyond routine banking and its diversification into newer areas of business that has given the bank a distinct identity. [8]

Future Plans

Though the growth of the bank was very fast during the seventies, it surpassed all previous records during early eighties. The increase in deposits during the last six-year period (1984-1990) was more than that achieved during the last five decades of working of the bank since inception.

The bank has got many first to its credit. True to the image of the trend setter in the industry, the bank has plans afoot to commence Consumer Banking, Portfolio Management, venture Capital, Mutual Fund, Corporate Counselling, Mergers and Acquisitions. A separate subsidiary for housing finance is also on the anvil.[9]

Vysya Bank is growing to meet the challenges of the changing needs around. It has a special place in the banking industry in the country. The bank is marching forward with its ideal to be the model financial institution which can offer total solutions to financial services needs.

The progress of Vysya Bank over 60 years is summed up in Table 2.10. The table presents slow and tiny steps at early stages i.e., till 1944 and a sharp raise during the year 1945 with a continued growth of deposits, advances and branches in further year till 1980's. Then there was a rapid increase of deposits, profit and advances. Especially from 1983 this steep raise is quite evident.

Notes :

1. Indira Gandhi Address to the Custodians of the Nationalised Banks in September, 1969.
2. Reserve Bank of India, Report on Trend and Progress of Banking in India, RBI, Bulletin, 1985–86, pp. 41–42.

Table 2.10 : Progress of Vysya Bank during 1933–1992

(Rs. in Lakhs)

Sr. No.	*Year*	*Paid Up Capital and Reserve Fund*	*Total Deposits*	*Total Advances*	*Net Proft*	*No. of Branches*	*No. of Employees*
1.	1931	0.71	1.06	1.53	0.0002	1	
2.	1932	0.81	1.59	2.05	0.04	1	
3.	1933	0.85	2.65	2.38	0.05	1	
4.	1934	0.88	3.75	4.24	0.04	2	
5.	1935	0.91	5.62	6.13	0.07	3	
6.	1936	0.93	6.70	5.26	0.006	3	
7.	1937	0.96	7.85	7.95	0.06	4	
8.	1938	0.99	6.80	6.79	0.03	4	
9.	1939	1.02	5.52	5.41	0.06	4	
10.	1940	1.02	3.90	3.78	0.01	4	
11.	1941	1.02	3.97	3.98	0.01	4	
12.	1942	1.02	6.01	5.70	0.10	4	
13.	1943	1.59	11.04	9.04	0.12	5	
14.	1944	3.33	16.02	13.99	0.16	6	
15.	1945	5.40	35.44	26.77	0.32	9	
16.	1946	10.30	50.97	39.29	0.55	15	
17.	1947	13.31	51.36	45.07	0.51	15	
18.	1948	13.40	53.74	31.02	0.47	15	
19.	1949	13.54	51.78	32.57	0.24	16	
20.	1950	13.59	52.49	38.02	0.85	16	
21.	1951	14.06	59.30	32.98	1.10	16	
22.	1952	13.89	64.81	27.18	0.68	16	
23.	1953	14.08	67.23	37.55	0.89	16	
24.	1954	14.27	77.05	39.12	0.90	16	
25.	1955	14.28	90.35	41.29	0.57	16	
26.	1956	14.47	98.49	48.57	0.90	16	
27.	1957	14.69	102.35	51.11	0.55	16	
28.	1958	14.91	112.77	69.64	1.07	16	
29.	1959	15.26	184.88	106.03	1.65	16	
30.	1960	15.88	200.97	135.00	1.31	19	

(Contd.)

Table 2.10 : (Contd.)

(Rs. in Lakhs)

Sr. No.	Year	Paid Up Capital and Reserve Fund	Total Deposits	Total Advances	Net Proft	No. of Branches	No. of Employees
31.	1961	16.38	207.66	133.78	1.19	19	
32.	1962	16.68	243.47	132.39	0.82	19	
33.	1963	16.98	281.46	164.42	0.81	21	
34.	1964	17.33	302.64	187.61	1.04	25	
35.	1965	17.65	354.25	208.16	0.30	27	
36.	1966	17.85	451.38	294.76	0.87	29	
37.	1967	18.50	562.18	300.30	1.55	29	
38.	1968	19.75	674.82	410.20	2.60	30	
39.	1969	23.80	829.75	494.78	3.79	36	
40.	1970	30.24	915.36	627.81	7.39	39	
41.	1971	34.66	1148.90	781.00	7.03	46	
42.	1972	36.03	1368.10	960.00	3.13	53	
43.	1973	36.55	1580.50	1127.10	2.18	61	
44.	1974	37.66	2035.33	1391.26	2.56	72	
45.	1975	47.90	3142.53	2109.85	16.43	90	
46.	1976	58.99	4811.05	3646.97	24.23	112	
47.	1977	75.61	6978.51	4430.64	23.96	150	
48.	1978	98.39	8575.46	5454.97	23.87	185	
49.	1979	110.39	11149.69	6216.69	20.38	210	
50.	1980	115.39	14142.73	8136.71	11.34	228	2650
51.	1981	135.59	17462.83	10522.04	12.93	236	2892
52.	1982	162.52	20483.62	12824.20	18.40	250	3010
53.	1983	178.78	24244.52	14591.90	23.46	257	3247
54.	1984	202.89	30877.30	17470.80	32.48	263	3408
55.	1985	352.93	40065.90	21728.22	100.02	268	3731
56.	1986	498.19	50779.30	26621.49	164.46	268	4062
57.	1987	778.19	61541.21	30809.58	253.65	275	4772
58.	1988–89	1161.27	71195.43	38080.06	419.85	283	4889
59.	1989–90	1621.27	85094.39	45847.59	503.46	289	4983
60.	1990–91		100430.00	53388.00	666.00	292	
61.	1991–92			77981.00		294	

Source : Diamond Jubilee Sovenir, The Vysya Bank Ltd.,

3. Diamond Jubliee Souvenir, Andhra Bank, 1983.
4. Diamond Jubliee Souvenir, Andhra Bank, 1983.
5. Diamond Jubilee Souvenir, The Vysya Bank, Ltd., p. 23.
6. Diamond Jubilee Souvenir, *Op. cit.*, p. 24.
7. Diamond Jubilee Souvenir, *Op. cit.*, p. 24.
8. Diamond Jubilee Souvenir, *Op. cit.*, p. 41.
9. Annual Report, 1991–92, Vysya Bank.

3

Research Design

Significance of Human Resource Management

The economic, social and cultural differences between developed and developing countries can mostly be attributed to the difference in human resource in those countries. In this context, Meier and Baldwin rightly points out, "Development does not occur spontaneously as a natural consequence when economic conditions are in some sense 'right', a catalyst, or agent is needed, and this require people with vision and drive".[1]

What was considered as just another factor of production among land, capital and management and was given a name 'labour' has gained such an importance that it is realised that nothing can be done without its cooperation and contribution even if there is abundant supply of other factors of production. Curle Adam, an economist puts it as "If underdeveloped countries have remained underdeveloped it is largely because the people are underdeveloped having no opportunity to realise their maximum potentialities".[2] As such the development of human resources is the key to the growth and development of nations.

Human resource management is a very vast area which covers almost all aspects of employee's work -life in an organisation right from the time when he enters into the organisation (recruitment) till he leaves it (retirement). Human resource management takes care of employee's economic, social and psychological needs. It also influences the social, political and cultural aspects of employee's life as organisational life is major part of the employee's life.

Recruitment, selection, induction, training and development, transfers, promotions, demotions, compensation package, working conditions that prevail are all part of human resource management. Apart from all these aspects, the area of 'Industrial Relations' is gaining importance. Many authors tend to make this area as vital part of human resource management.

Many new concepts and trends are taking place in Human Resource Management and are gaining importance. One such important concept is 'Quality of Work Life'. Though the importance of quality of work life was realised long ago, its practice is being stressed upon and specific title is being given only recently. Since then, this term is being used extensively by employees, employers, Government and academicians.

Quality of Work Life

Rosow (1974) explains the importance of work and relates it to success or failure of a man in his society. According to him, "Work is the core of life, considering the deeper meaning of work to be individual and to life's values, work means being a good provider, it means autonomy, it pays off its success and it establishes self-respect or self-worth within this framework. The person who openly confesses active job dissatisfaction is virtually admitting failure as a man, a failure in fulfilling his moral role in society".[3]

Richard Walton (1979) had taken up extensive research on quality of work life. He can be considered as a major contributor to this concept who devised eight-point criteria to measure QWL. According to him "Quality of Work Life is a work culture that serves as the corner stone".[4] He says that the work culture of an organisation should be recognised and improved to improve quality of work life of that organisation.

One of the reasons for the growing importance of QWL could be realisation on the part of employees about their rights, growing unionism and increasing level of formal education of employees. They are united now than ever. Each and every worker tends to join some union or the other, for their own protection and well-being. Unions put all their efforts into educate their workers and make them realise their rights and as to what they can expect from the management in return to what they contribute. Though monetary benefits still occupy first place in the list of elements of QWL, other elements like physical working conditions, job restructuring and redesign, career development, promotional opportunities etc., are gaining importance rapidly. As such the workers expect management to improve all these facilities which thereby improve QWL.

QWL emerged to end exploitation and injustice on the part of employees. As De points out "QWL is an indicator of how free the society is from exploitation, injustice, inequality, oppression and restrictions on the continuity of growth of man, leading to his development to the fullest."[5]

The evolution of the concept QWL has been in three phases—Scientific management movement, Human relations movement and socio-technical movement. Thus, 'the importance of quality of work life was realised as early as Taylor's scientific management movement'.

Quality of work life is more than simple a concept, a means or an end. According to Johnson Alexander and Robin[6], quality of work life embodies the following interrelated sets of ideas.

- Ideas dealing with body of knowledge, concept and experiences related to the nature, meaning and structure of work.
- Ideas dealing with nature and process of introducing and managing organisational change, and
- Ideas dealing with outcome or results of the change process.

Significance of QWL in Service-Oriented Industries

Service organisations play a vital role in our economy in terms of the creation of employment potential and contribution to the national income. The involvement and role of human resource of in-service organisation is very high as entire process of rendering service is their responsibility. As such improving QWL in service organisation to secure best possible performance from employees has become very important.

Commercial banks are an important part of service organisations in countries like India. In a planned economy like ours the part played by banks is very significant. The commercial banks in

India supply credit to the promotional and developmental activities of the society and at the same time restrict credit for socially undesirable, unwanted and economically less beneficial purposes. Thus commercial banks help the Government in implementing the long term plans and for utilising the credit according to the planned priorities of the country.

The spectrum of Commercial banks has grown remarkably . especially in the post nationalisation period. Commercial banks evolved various modes and instruments of financing moving away from traditional banking to social banking and from class banking to mass banking by responding to socio-economic needs of the public. The commercial banks have to face challenges due to the liberalisation policy.

As such the banking industry needs human resources if with intelligence, logical sense and quick grasping. Apart from these aspects, most importantly banking industry needs motivated personnel with entrepreneurial flair, financial wizard, technical brilliance, administrative efficiency etc. In fact, sound QWL enables the bank management to have such human resources. The study of quality of work life in commercial Bank assumes greater significance in view of economic liberalisation and need for qualitative human resources.

Review of Literature

There are significant number of books and periodicals which enable us understand and comprehend the concept Human Resource Management. There is a reference about the Quality of Work Life in these books. P. Subba Rao,[7] in his book on 'personnel/ Human Resource Management, analysed the conceptual issues on QWL.

There are some studies in the area of human resource management in banking industry which have indirect bearing on QWL in banks.

Subba Rao, P.[8] conducted a study on impact of various factors on job satisfaction on different employees. Baldev R. Sharma[9] also conducted a study on "Human Resource Management in Banking Industry" where impact of managerial beliefs and work technology on organisational climate and management have been discussed. Ramesh Gelli,[10] in his paper on "Participative

Management: Quality Circles Application to Banking" discussed various techniques for application of participative management and quality circles. Udai Pareek,[11] in his paper on "Introducing HRD in Banks" explains the improvement of HRD climate, strategy and spirit for implementation of HRD techniques in banks. Subba Rao, P.[12] discusses role of bank manager as counsellor and his action plan in his paper on "Bank Branch Manager as a Counsellor".

Though there are no books available on Quality of Work Life, a limited number of studies were conducted in this area. Seashore Stanley E.[13] had presented impact of job satisfaction on quality of employment in social indications research. Stanley[14] also assessed the experience of U.S. in this regard. Taylor J.C.[15] had examined various dimensions of quality of working life.

The major researches in this field are Sinha and Sayeed (1982) and Mehta (1984 & 1985) and Taylor (1974). They all assumed that the quality of work life of entire organisation can be summed up through individual experiences.

There are also number of papers presented on quality of work life. Rosow J.M.[16] in his article on Quality of Work Life - Issues for the 1980s—reviews recent trends of QWL. Singh J.P.[17] explains QWL, its significance and feasibility in Indian context in his article on 'Improving QWL in the Indian Context'. P.Singh[18] brings out the impact of two interrelated components of employee work life motivation and QWL in his study on "Motivational Profile and Quality of Corporate Work Life: A Case of Mismatch. Thorsrud, E.[19] brings out comprehensive comparison between QWL in first and Third World countries in his paper on 'QWL in the First and the Third World'. Walton R.E.[20] has written many papers exclusively on various components of QWL. In one such paper on "ideas for Action—Improving the Quality of Work" he discusses in detail practicality and various techniques to be practiced for successful implementation of QWL.

Mehta, P.[21] who had put in considerable research in the field of QWL, discussed in his paper on 'Rising Aspirations, Quality of Life and Work Organisation' discusses QWL from the point of view of workers and tries to match QWL to their changing attitudes. Maccoby, M[22] on the other hand extends the perview of QWL to management also. In his article on 'Helping Labour and Management Set-up Quality of Work Life Programme' makes various suggestions to both workers and management for practice of QWL.

Some of the most famous organisations of the World practised QWL in their organisations successfully. These success stories are brought out by some of the authors. R.F. Graver[23] in his study 'At & T QWL Experiment - A Practical case Study' and R.H. Guest[24] in his study on 'Quality of Work Life—Learning from Terrytown, brings out experiences of At & T and Terrytown. S.K. Karla and S. Ghosh[25] in their article on 'Quality of Work Life: Some Determinants' reviews various components of QWL. N. Ahmed[26] in his article on 'Quality of Work Life: A need for Understanding', stressed on good understanding of the concept 'Quality of Work Life' to avoid vagueness. K.C.D. Souza[27] in his article on QWL: An Evolutionary Perspective' discusses QWL as an emerging concept with various new areas taking place in it from time to time. C.L. Cooper[28] especially talks about various factors which influence QWL of Mangers in his paper on 'The Quality of Managerial Life—The stresses and Satisfiers'. F. Friedlander and M. Newton,[29] assess the impact of QWL on job satisfaction.

The analysis of review of literature clears that though there are some studies on QWL in manufacturing organisations in India and other countries, studies on QWL in service organisations in general and commercial banks in particular are rare to find.

Need for the Study

Special attention is to be paid towards the studies on service oriented organisation which play vital role in liberalised economy. Commercial banks are one such major service oriented organisations where there is a dearth of research studies on QWL. Hence, it is felt that there is a greater need for a study on QWL in commercial banks. As such an attempt is made to conduct a study on QWL in commercial banks in public and private sectors.

Objectives of the Study

The present study is conducted with the objectives :

1. To enquire into the economic and employment aspects of Quality of Work Life in Andhra Bank which is a public sector bank and the Vysya Bank Ltd., a private sector bank;
2. To study the quality of work life in terms of social aspects in Andhra Bank and The Vysya Bank Ltd.;

3. To evaluate QWL in terms of the development of human capabilities, career planning and development, nature of work, organisational structure etc. in Andhra Bank and The Vysya Bank Ltd.;
4. To evaluate the practices of QWL in Andhra Bank and The Vysya Bank Ltd., and other suggestions for improvement of QWL in both the banks in particular and banking industry in general.

The head office of Andhra Bank at Hyderabad and head office of Vysya Bank, Bangalore were visited to gather information regarding data on growth and development of both the banks and practices of human resources management in both the banks. Andhra Bank Staff Training College at Hyderabad and Vysya Bank Staff Training College at Bangalore were also visited to gather training content and other secondary information regarding these banks.

Much of the conceptual information regarding QWL has been gathered from libraries of Sri Krishnadevaraya University and University of Calcutta and Indian Institute of Management, Ahmedabad, National Labour Institute, Delhi and Sri Krishnadevaraya Institute of Management.

The Primary data are collected from management and employee respondents of both the banks. Three different types of questionnaires are structured to circulate among three types of respondents of commercial banks viz., employees, management and members of trade unions. The primary data are mainly gathered through questionnaires and interview method has also been used wherever necessary to assess the rich experiences of employees and managers. Information from trade union members has also been gathered through interviews. However, members of trade unions reflected similar opinions as that of employees as almost all employees are members of trade unions. As such views of employees and management are being stressed for analysis.

As the nature of business, functions, practices of human resource management, conditions of work are similar in commercial banks, it is decided to study QWL in two banks. One from public sector and another from private sector. Steps are taken to select a representative bank from among the public sector which can also be comparable with private sector bank. Andhra Bank from public sector banks satisfies these requirements. As such, Andhra Bank is selected for the purpose of the study. Similarly steps are also taken to select one bank from private sector which represents the private sector banks, and comparable with public sector banks as closest as possible. The Vysya Bank Ltd., from private sector banks, is selected for the study as it satisfies the requirements. Thus Andhra Bank and the Vysya Bank Ltd., are selected as sample banks for the study.

Further, the employees and managers of these banks may have similar experiences about the Quality of Work Life. Hence, a sample of 1.5 per cent of employees and 2 per cent of managers is selected on stratified random sampling basis to collect the opinions and views of respondents about various aspects of QWL. The number of employees of Andhra Bank by the end of March 1991 is 15,604. A sample of 1.5 per cent i.e., 236 were selected from different categories of employees like clerks, cashiers and typists maintaining 1.5 per cent from each category. Similarly a sample of 113 respondents are selected from all categories (1.5%) out of 4,313 employees of Vysya Bank as on March 31, 1991.

Similarly, a sample of 2 per cent from managers of these two banks is selected on the basis of stratified random sample techniques maintaining 2 per cent sample from different categories of managers like Junior, middle and senior management. A sample of 113 management respondents out of 5,355 managers of Andhra Bank and a sample of seven respondents out of 327 managers of Vysya Bank are selected to collect the primary data.

Views of sample members are assessed on a five-point scale from which weighted average values of total sample is calculated. Based on the weighed average values, satisfaction levels of respondents are measured as 2 for absolutely positive, 1 for positive, 0 for neutral, –1 for negative and –2 for absolutely negative.

Scope of the Study and Presentation

The present study reflects existing quality of work life of Andhra bank and Vysya Bank. To measure QWL in these banks, Walton's eight-point criterion consisting of adequate and fair compensation, safe and healthy working conditions, opportunity to use and develop human capabilities, opportunity for career growth, social integration in work force, constitutionalism in the work organisation, work and quality of life and social relevance of work are used. Apart from these, components like influence of family, trade unions and organisations structure, which are considered as important in Indian context, are also being measured.

The study is presented in eight chapters. The concept of QWL, evolution of the concept since scientific management phase and its significance at present are discussed in Chapter 1.

The evolution and growth of banking industry in general and Andhra Bank and the Vysya Bank Ltd., in particular are presented in Chapter 2. The Research Design of the Study is presented in Chapter 3.

Economic aspects of QWL are presented in Chapter 4. Employment conditions, including all physical facilities, are presented in Chapter 5. Social aspects, including social integration inside organisation and social relevance of work, influence of family and Trade Unions and constitutionalism, are presented in Chapter 6. Human Resource Development aspects comprising of developing human capabilities, career planning and growth, work and its impact on QWL and other aspects like organisational structure and influence of work on QWL are presented in Chapter 7. Finally the evaluation and suggestions of the study are presented in Chapter 8.

Limitations of the Study

An academic study of this nature has had limitation in view of restricted access to research and the general confidential nature of working of banks. This limitation, however, was reduced to a great extent through interview method. Another limitation is that, there were problem in soliciting views of employees and managers through structured questionnaire as many employees tend to avoid extremes and take neutral stand regarding many aspects. Reaching at a conclusion becomes difficult in such case. This limitation was, however, reduced through informal discussions with the employees and managers. Lastly, it is difficult to an individual to draw up an accurate picture of quality of work life of employees divided into various categories scattered geographically all over the country and particularly in rural areas under different circumstances, perceptions, attitudes etc. However, every effort is made to gather and evaluate the situation as accurately and objectively as possible.

Notes :

1. Meier Gerold, M., and Baldwin Robert, E. 'Economic Development Theory, History and Policy', John Wiley and Sons, New York, 1967, p. 299.
2. Curle Adam, 'Some Aspects of Educational Planning in Underdeveloped Areas', Harward Business Review, Vol. 3, Summer, 1962, p. 300.
3. Rosow J.M., 'Quality of Working Life and Productivity : The Double Pay off : paper presented at Conference of the American Institute Inc., Illiois, April, 77.
4. Walton, R.E., 'Ideas for Action—Improving the Quality of Work Life'. Harward Business Review, May–June, 1974. pp. 58–59.
5. De, N.R., 'Interlinkage Between QWL and QL', Productivity, 1982, 22 (4), p. 87.
6. Johnson, Carl P. Alexander, Mark and Robin, "Quality of Working Life : The Idea and Its Application", Canada, 1978.
7. P. Subba Rao and V.S.P. Rao, op. cit.
8. Subba Rao, P. "Principles and Practices of Bank Management", Himalaya Publications, Bombay, 1988.
9. Baldev R. Sharma, "Human Resource Management in Banking Industry".
10. Ramesh Gelli, "Quality Circles Application to Banking", Anil K. Kandelwal (Ed.) "Human Resource Development in Banks", Oxford and IBH Publishing Co. (P) Ltd., New Delhi.
11. Udai Pareek, "Introducing HRD in Banks", in "Human Resource Development, Anmol Publications, New Delhi, 1991 p. 156.
12. Subba Rao, P. "Bank Branch Manager as a Counsellor", State Bank of India Monthly Review, Vol. XXV, No. 10, Oct. 1986, pp. 494–496.
13. Seashore Stanely, E. Job Satisfaction as an Indicator of the Quality of Employment, Social Indications Research, 1974, 1 (2), pp. 135–168.
14. Seashore Stanely, E. Assessing the Quality of Working Life, The U.S. Experience, Labour and Society, 1976, 1(2), pp. 69–79.
15. Taylor J.C. An Emperical examination of the Dimensions of Quality of Working Life, Centre for Quality of Working Life, Institute of Industrial Relations, University of California, Los Angles, (1) 1977.
16. Rosow J.M. Quality of Work Life Issues for the 1980s, Training and Development Journal, March 1988, pp. 33–52.
17. Singh J.P. Improving QWL in Indian Context, Productivity, Vol. 22 (4), 1982, pp. 13–20.

18. Singh, P. Motivational Profile & Quality of Corporate Work Life : A Case of Mismatch, Indian Management, February, 1984, pp. 13–20.

19. Throsrud, E. QWL in the First and Third World, Productivity Vol. 22 (4), 1982, pp. 3–11.

20. Walton R.E. 'Ideas for Action—Improving the Quality of Work Life, Harward Business Review, May–June 1974, pp. 58–59.

21. Mehta, P. 'Rising Aspirations, Quality of Life and Work Organisation', Productivity, 22(4), 1982, pp. 86–88.

22. Maecoby, M. Helping Labour and Mangement set-up Quality of Work Life Program, Monthly Labour Review March, 1984, pp. 1–5.

23. Graver, R.F. 'At & T' QWL Experiment—A Practical Case Study, Management Review, June 1983, pp. 12–16.

24. Guert, R.H. Quality of Work Life—Learning from Terrytown, Hardward Business Review, July–August, 1979, pp. 28–29.

25. Karla, S.K. and Ghosh, S, "Quality of Work Life : Some Determinants, Indian Management, Sept., 1983, pp. 19–21.

26. Ahmed, N. Quality of Work Life : A Need for Understand", Indian Management, Vol. 20 (11), 1981, pp. 29–33.

27. D'Souza, K.C., QWL : An Evolutionary Perspective, Abhigyan, Autumn, 1984, pp. 1–15.

28. Cooper C.L., 'The Quality of Managerial Life—The Stressors and Satisfiers', Advanced Management Education, 1980, pp. 9–20.

29. Friendlander, F. and Newton, M. 'Multiple Impact of Organisational Climate and Individual Value System upon Job Satisfaction, Personnel Psychology, Vol. 22, 1969.

4

Economic Aspects of Quality of Work Life

Introduction

Economic aspects of employee's work life play a very important role in motivating the employees. It is so especially in countries like India, where most of the population is still around poverty line and most of the middle level employees are still striving for fair standard of living. But the other aspects like social and work culture are rapidly gaining importance. However, the monetary benefits still occupy first place in the list of employee's preference.

Quality of work life is basically the Quality of life that an employee experiences at his work place. Unless good quality of work life is provided to an employee, he cannot be motivated towards work. Quality of work life covers all aspects of employee's work life like economic, social, psychological and organisational. Among these aspects, economic aspects occupy first place. Walton, promoter of QWL, also gives first place to the monetary benefits in his eight-point criteria measure QWL. The importance of monetary benefits prevail in both manufacturing as well as service oriented industries like banks.

Andhra Bank is one of the biggest public sector banks with employee's strength of 15,604 (1991–'92). The emoluments paid to its employees are shown in Table 4.1. It is observed from the table that total amount of salaries increased from Rs. 42.89 crores to Rs. 75.77 crores during 1987-'88 and 1992.

Table 4.1 : Amount of Salary Paid to the Employees of Andhra Bank during 1987–92

(Rs. in Crores)

Year	*Total Amount of Salaries*
1987–88	42.89
1988–89	66.18
1989–90	66.04
1990–91	67.46
1991–92	75.77

Source : Records of Andhra Bank, Hyderabad.

Apart from salaries, Andhra Bank also provides various fringe benefits to its employees like provident fund, bonus, local travelling concession, pension scheme etc. Expenditure on fringe benefits during 1991 and 1992 are shown in Table 4.2

As far as the salaries are concerned, the employees of Andhra Bank come under various scales. Mostly the salaries are fixed according to the rules and norms of Bank's Regulatory Board.

Table 4.2 : Amount of Leave Benefit paid to the Employees of Andhra Bank during 1991–92

(Rs. in Crores)

S. No.	*Particulars*	*1991*	*1992*
1.	Leave encashment	0.84	1.11
2.	Overtime Wages	–	0.04
3.	Incentives for Family Planning	0.02	0.10
4.	Provident Fund	4.02	4.04
5.	Bonus paid	0.90	0.62
6.	Gratuity and Group Insurance	4.44	1.23
7.	Peon's Uniform	–	0.15
8.	T.A., D.A. and L.F.C.	–	1.22
9.	Miscellaneous entertainment	–	0.18

Source : Records of Andhra Bank, Hyderabad.

There are seven scales. These scales are applicable to officers, junior, senior and top managers. Apart form these levels of managers, there are award and sub staff. The staff whose salaries are decided based upon the negotiations, between management and unions, are summarised and presented in Table 4.3.

Table 4.3 : Pay Scale of Officers and Managers of Andhra Bank (With effect from 1st January, 1987)

Scales	*Employees covered*	*Salaries in Rs.*
Scale I	Officers	2100–120/16–4020
Scale II	Senior Manager	3060–120/10–4260–130/1–4390
Scale III	Middle, Senior and Top Manager	4020–120/2–4260–130/5 4910 (1.11.89)
Scale IV	Middle, Senior and Top Manager	4520–130/3–4910–140/1 5050–150/2–5350
Scale V	Middle, Senior and Top Manager	5200–150/5–5950
Scale VI	Middle, Senior and Top Manager	5800–150/5–6550
Scale VII	Middle, Senior and Top Manager	6400–150/4–7000

Source : Records of Andhra Bank, Hyderabad.

Vysya Bank is a private sector bank. It earned a prestigious image[1]. Vysya Bank is known for its efficient and smooth operation and its customer service among the private sector banks[2]. It is operating with 4,314 employees. The amount of salary paid by Vysya Bank to its employees towards basic, D.A., bonus and other allowances is summarised and presented in Table 4.4.

It is observed from the table that the basic pay of the employees has increased from Rs. 7.30 lakhs to Rs. 11.71 lakhs during 1988-89 and 1990-91. Apart from salaries, Vysya Bank is also taking many steps towards welfare of its employees by providing other benefits like leave fare, medical aid and productivity bonus etc. The amount paid towards leave fare during January 1, 1987 and December 21, 1991 is shown in Table 4.5.

Table 4.4 : Salaries Paid to the Employees of Vysya Bank during 1988–1989 to 1990–1991

(Rs. in thousands)

S.No.	*Particulars*	*1-1-1988-89*	*1989-90*	*1990-91*
1.	Basic	730.12	1276.08	1171.20
2.	Dearness Allowance	762.46	318.44	624.68
3.	Other Allowances	40.54	34.03	52.40
4.	Bonus	44.85	51.16	138.07

Source : Records of Vysya Bank, Bangalore.

Table 4.5 : Leave Fare for Employees of Vysya Bank during 1987–1991

S.No.	*Period*	*No. of employees availing benefit*	*Amount (in Rs.)*
1.	1-1-1987 to 31-12-1987	1241	2133608.35
2.	1-1-1988 to 31-03-1989	1340	2705667.12
3.	1-4-1989 to 31-03-1990	1100	2369593.55
4.	1-4-1990 to 31-03-1991	812	2053334.72

Source : Records of Vysya Bank, Bangalore.

Quality of work life also denotes the feelings of employees and management in addition to the facilities provided by the Management. Against this background, an attempt is made to analyse the views of management and employees representatives to find out the level of feelings about the salaries and fringe benefits.

The opinions collected from respondents of management, employees and trade unions with the help of structured questionnaires are analysed by way of adopting values (+2, +1, 0, –1, –2) from most positive to most negative values of five statements for each question respectively. Based upon these calculations the collective opinions of the sample members is decided as to whether absolutely positive, positive, neutral negative and absolutely negative respectively. The ascertained values from management and employees are presented in Table 4.6 and 4.7 respectively.

Table 4.6 : Andhra Bank Management Representatives Opinions on Salaries of Employees

Opinion of Management on Salaries	*Weighted Average Value*
Salary in comparison with other banks	+ 0.96
Salary in comparison with other financial institutions	+ 0.37
Salary in comparison with ability of management	+ 0.48
Salary in comparison with cost of living of employees	+ 0.75
Total salary meeting needs of employees	+ 0.80

Source : Primary Data.

Table 4.7 : Andhra Bank Employees Opinion about their Salry

Opinion of Employees on Salaries	*Weighted Average Value*
Adequacy of basic pay	+ 0.55
Adequacy of House Rent Allowance	– 2.40
Adequacy of Dearness Allowance	+ 0.05
Adequacy of Total Salary	+ 0.48

Source : Primary Data.

Views of Management of Andhra Bank

It is observed from these tables that the representatives of management consider the pay scales of its employees, when compared to the employees of other banks positive, as the weighted average is +0.96 (close to +1). They justify themselves what they pay to their employees.

But the management respondents didn't express positive opinion regarding the salary when compared to that of the employees of the financial institutions like IDBI, IFCI and NABARD as the weighted average score is 0.37 which is far from +1. Similar options were expressed by the management respondents regarding comparison between pay scales and bank's ability to pay i.e., no positive opinion was expressed. The score of weighted average is +0.48 which is above the score of comparison with other financial institutions.

Cost of living of employees is another important aspect which influences the attitudes of employees towards their salary. Management also makes attempts to adjust pay scales according to the changes in cost of living from time to time. As such attempts were made to collect opinions from management respondents regarding adequacy of salary in view of raising living cost. The weighted average of the opinions of management respondents is moderate (+0.75).

Employees mostly concern about the adequacy of the total salary to meet their various needs like living, children's education, medical aid and the like Employees are satisfied with the job and feel happy, if their salaries are adequate to meet their requirements and the vice versa is true, if the salaries are not adequate. Management's opinions are collected to findout whether their salaries are adequate to meet employees requirements or not.

It is observed from the table that majority of respondents of management (66) viewed that the salaries are adequate to meet all needs of employees. The weighted average of the views of management is +0.80. Thus the management feel that the salary of their employees meet their needs to some extent though not completely. They are little more positive in this aspect than that of salary compared to the cost of living of employees (+0.75).

The positive opinion expressed by management representatives in case of the salaries compared to that of other banks can be attributed to the fact that most of the banks follow the scales suggested by 'Banks Regulatory Board'. As such there is not much deviation in the scales drawn by the employees of various banks. Whereas they have not been that positive compared to those of other financial institutions (weighted average being +0.37). This opinion is due to the reason that the ability of financial institutions to pay would be higher than that of the banks. It is interesting to observe that the management has felt that the salaries compared to the ability of management respondents (54), tend to express a neutral answer i.e., they are neither positive nor negative. As such when compared to the fair financial position of the bank they do not quite agree with the fairness of the salaries of their employees. However, management has felt that the salaries of employees meet their need mostly, in spite of their inadequacy who compared to the salaries of other financial institutions and ability of management to pay. The management still feels that the salaries of employees meet their needs, though they are not absolutely positive (weighted average being +0.80).

Attitude of Employees of Andhra Bank

The economic aspects play all the more important role in moulding the attitude of the employees towards their work. Though many of the respondents were reluctant to mention their exact salaries, they were more cooperative to express their view when asked about adequacy of Basic, D.A., HRA and total salary on five point scale. The sample chosen here is mostly of clerical grade. A sample of 236 employees were chosen.

Salary of an employe consists of various components like basic, D.A., HRA, etc. An attempt is made to find out the views of employees regarding adequacy of these components to meet their needs at which they are aimed. Basic pay is meant to meet needs of employees except house rent. Basic needs of employees are food and clothing and other needs like education of children, their marriage and other comforts etc. The weighted average of opinions ascertained from employees is 0.55, which is little above than half of positive value +1. As such the employees though tend towards positive side, it is only to some extent. So, it can be said that basic pay according to the employees meets their needs to an extent of 55 per cent.

House Rent Allowance is another important component of total salary. HRA is paid to meet the house rent expenditure of employees. This aspect assumes more importance as majority of employees are put up at suburban and urban areas, where the house rents are usually high. The weighted average value of opinions ascertained here is –2.4 which is absolutely negative. Understandably, the HRA paid by bank to various categories of employees, particularly to award staff cannot meet the requirements of employees towards house rent. Employees of clerical grade are mostly paid around Rs. 200 towards HRA where as the rent of a moderate house in any suburban or urban areas is not less than Rs. 800.

Dearness Allowance is paid especially to meet the raising cost of living. The basic pay is fixed at long intervals and the cost of living is ever increasing. DA is paid to compensate expenditure of raising living cost. To find out how far does this amount really serve the purpose, employees have been asked to measure its adequacy with the help of five-point scale ranging from most positive to most negative.

Majority of employee i.e., 96 out of 236 are neutral regarding this aspect. As a result the weighted average is +0.05. The trend is above neutral to an extent of just 0.05. DA in banks usually amounts to around 75 per cent of employees basic pay. Still the employees are mostly neutral in comparing their DA with real needs, not either satisfied or dissatisfied.

Total salary is mostly the concern of employees. When one talks about his salary, it is always his gross salary. As such apart from gathering opinions about how far various components meet the needs, their view point about total salary meeting the needs is also found out. According to them, total salary meets their needs to an extent of 48 per cent the ascertained weighted average value being +0.48, which is almost half towards positive +1.

The most important aspect of quality of work life i.e., the monetary benefits of the employee meet half of the actual needs. Employees are much dissatisfied with the HRA that is paid. Regarding D.A. they are almost neutral. It is important to note here that this aspect affects the employees attitudes towards QWL and their morale and motivation.

Trade Unions form an important part of work force. This is especially so, in case of commercial bank as almost all employees are trade union members. In a sample of 235 in Andhra Bank, 197 employees are the members of trade unions. 20 of them are not members of any union and 9 of them did not respond. So, the Trade Unions naturally play a very important role in the affairs of the bank, including maintenance of quality of work life. An attempt is made to meet as many trade union members are possible and record their view points. Their opinions are gathered with the help of structured questionnaire which contains mostly open end questions. Since they cannot be quantified, analysis is done based on the descriptive responses that they have given. The most prominent unions in the bank are Andhra Bank Award Staff Employees Union, All India Bank Employee Association and All India Bank Officer's Conference. The award staff employees union is affiliated to All India Bank Employees Association.

The trade union members are asked about their opinion regarding adequacy of various components of QWL provided to them bank. They are also asked to mention the reasons for dissatisfaction. If they are dissatisfied about the QWL, they are asked to specify action taken by the unions to improve the QWL and the means adopted for this purpose.

Regarding monetary benefits, respondents have been either neutral or positive. Mostly they have been positive, some of them have been neutral. But none have been negative. Still, they have opined that their unions are working towards improving the monetary benefits of the employees, the means adopted have been basically negotiations. It is assumed that unions in general are not very discontented with the management as far as monetary benefits are concerned. They could so far solve whatever problem they had in this regard mostly through negotiations.

Comparison of viewpoints of management, employees and trade union members also provides an interesting insight. While the management has felt that total emoluments meet the real needs of employees to an extent of 80 per cent, employees felt it is only 48 per cent of the requirements. As many as 75 per cent of the sample trade union members are positive regarding their pay scales meeting their requirements. There is a gap of around 30 per cent in what the management and employees think about the emoluments. This gap can be attributed to the fact that requirements of the employees vary from the estimations of management. What employees feel as basic requirements may not be felt by the management. With the rapid changing way of life in society, comforts become necessities and luxuries become comforts. What might have been viewed by management as luxurious way of life might have been considered as just comfortable way of life by employees.

The management might take a four-member family as a standard. But the employee, whose family members are more than four will have problems with adjusting to the available pay scales. In fact 80 per cent of the respondent employees have more than four dependents and sometimes the number crossed even seven. Interestingly none of the employees stated that they have no dependents. As many as 95 per cent of employees even in the age group of less than thirty are married. Due to the phenomena of early marriage in our country an employee has dependents right form the time when he joins his job. If it is a joint family, the number of dependents is more than three. As such there is not much scope for an employee for savings. It is struggle for existence right from the beginning. This aspect might have been overseen by the management.

Another reason for the dissatisfaction of employees could be the extra expenditure that they have to bear due to regional differences. It is important to note here that Andhra Bank is not paying 'City Compensatory Allowance'. As such those who are placed in urban areas find it difficult to cope up with the ever increasing costs. The HRA paid by the bank is also not quite sufficient to employees which was reflected in their giving absolutely negative opinion (–2) in this regard.

But Andhra Bank considers in its transfer and placement policy, the place of work of the spouse/while transferring/placing an employee. This reduces the double expenditure that it is to be spent by them. Employees in informal interviews with them expressed their satisfaction over this aspect.

To sum up, management, employees and trade unions have positive opinions regarding monetary aspects provided by Andhra Bank to an extent of around 50 per cent.

Vysya Bank is the biggest bank in private sector known not only for its customer service and efficiency but also for its concern for employee's welfare. To compare the attitudes of management, employees and representatives of trade unions, opinions are collected through structured questionnaires from the chosen sample and weighted average of their opinions are derived and presented in Table 4.8 and 4.9.

Vysya Bank Managements Perception

The representatives of management expressed that they pay fair salaries when compared to the other banks. The weighted average value that is ascertained is +0.85 which is close to positive +1. Regarding comparison with other financial institutes, though majority of respondents have been on positive side, there are also equal number of employees who were neutral and negative. As such, the weighted average value that is ascertained is neutral 'O'.

Table 4.8 : Vysya Bank Management Representatives Opinion on Salaries of Employees

Opinion of Management on Salaries	*Weighted Average Value*
Salary in comparison with other banks	+ 0.85
Salary in comparison with other financial institutions	+ 0.00
Salary in comparison with the ability of management	+ 1.70
Salary in comparison with the cost of living of employees	+ 0.70
Total salary meeting needs of employees	+ 0.25

Source : Primary Data.

Table 4.9 : Vysya Bank Employees Opinion on their Salary

Opinion of Employees on Salaries	*Weighted Average Value*
Adequacy of basic pay	+ 0.62
Adequacy of House Rent Allowance	– 0.81
Adequacy of Dearness Allowance	+ 0.07
Adequacy of Total Salary	+ 0.09

Source : Primary Data.

Salaries in comparison with ability of management to pay are nearer to absolute positive value +2 (+1.70). The respondents are mostly satisfied with what they pay to employees when compared to their ability. Cost of living of employees is another aspect to which salaries are compared. Here again the opinions of representatives of management are almost positive (0.70).

But interestingly in spite of being positive, while comparing salaries with other banks, financial institutions, their own ability and employee's cost of living, they are not very positive as far as total salary is concerned. The weighted average value ascertained is +0.28, which is less than half of positive value +1. So the representatives of management feel that the total salary meet the needs of employees only to some extent.

Vysya Bank Employee's Views

The employees of Vysya Bank feel more or less as that of the management. The employees are mostly positive regarding various aspects of their salary. Majority of respondents from employees i.e., 30 of 64 are neutral about adequacy of their basic pay. But rest of them are either positive or absolutely positive. The weighted average value thus calculated is +0.62.

House Rent Allowance is one aspect regarding which the employees are not satisfied. They are almost negative in their opinion. The weighted average ascertained here is –0.81.

The aspects about which the employees are nearly neutral are 'Dearness Allowance' and 'Total Salary'. Regarding dearness allowance majority of the employees are either neutral or negative. Same is the case with the total salary, the weighted average of which is +0.09 which is close to '0'.

Trade unions of Vysya Bank also have an important role to play in protecting the economic as well as social interests of their members. Most of the employees are members of trade unions. Some of the members of trade union were asked about the adequacy of salaries that are being paid to employees. The respondents were mostly positive about adequacy. But some of them complained that the management is not taking, raising cost of living into account while fixing up the pay structure.

The management and employees of Vysya Bank share similar views regarding monetary aspect. Trade union members also are largely satisfied with financial aspect. It can be seen that the respondents from employees side are mostly positive as far as basic and H.R.A. are concerned. The management is also positive while comparing their employee's salary with that of other banks and financial institutions.

As far as total salary is concerned both the parties take a neutral stand. This trend has some psychological implications. Though one is satisfied with various components of his pay he still aspires for more, another is never satisfied with what he receives by way of monetary benefits immaterial of what he receives. It is the human tendency to express dissatisfaction or atleast be neutral when directly asked about his pay. But the members of trade unions have pin-pointed the aspect of management neglecting to take cost of living into account. This is also reflected in the opinions of employees. They were mostly neutral when asked about the adequacy of dearness allowance. Cost of living again is a subjective issue about which both management and employees/ trade union members may have different opinions. Andhra Bank and Vysya Bank are conscious of quality of work life of their employees. Both the banks are working towards improving quality of work life of their employees, when the opinions of management and employees of both the banks are compared with each other regarding the monetary benefits which forms an important and first part of quality of work life there were some interesting insights.

The management of Andhra Bank is more satisfied and confident that what they pay is fair when compared to other banks, financial institutions, their ability to pay and the cost of living of employees. Whereas the management of Vysya Bank is not that confident. They are mostly neutral. In case of total salary when the weighted average of the opinion of management of Andhra Bank are close to +1 i.e., +0.80. The same value in case of management of Vysya Bank is close to neutral i.e., +0.28.

The employees of both the banks share similar views regarding various components of their salaries. The employees of Andhra Bank are absolutely negative regarding HRA they receive whereas the employees of Vysya Bank are negative. In case of basic and DA they express mostly positive opinions, with little deviations.

Regarding total salary, the employees of Vysya Bank are more dissatisfied than that of the employees of Andhra Bank.

The trade union members of both the banks do not differ much with each other. Though generally satisfied with the monetary benefits they receive, they asked for restructuring of compensation time and again.

Among various components of salary, HRA is cause of concern as employes of both the banks gave negative opinions. As such managements of both the banks may take steps for increase in H.R.A. taking into account the enhanced house rents.

In case of Vysya Bank, both management and employees expressed their dissatisfaction regarding their salaries. As the management realise the inadequacy of salary they can take necessary steps to restructure it.

It is concluded that all parties of the organisation i.e., management employees and trade unions are generally satisfied with their salaries except H.R.A. H.R.A. occupies an important part of monetary benefits because home is a place where employees relax after busy bank hours. If he cannot afford a comfortable house with good facilities, it affects his work life. As an employee should be provided with good facilities for effective work, he should also be provided facilities to relax. As such managements of both the banks should take steps to increase HRA to their employees. The trade unions, though have some minor problems are confident of solving them by way of negotiations. Comparatively, the management and employees of Andhra Bank are more positive in their opinions regarding various aspects of monetary benefits than the management and employees of Vysya Bank. Hence it is suggested that the management of Vysya Bank should take steps to make the employees feel satisfied with the important part of QWL i.e., monetary aspects.

Notes :

1. 'Vysya bank Foray into Housing', *Financial Express*, Nov. 26, 1989.
2. 'Committed to Excellence', Corporate Reports, *Business India*, April 16–28, 1991.

5

Working Conditions

Introduction

Quality of work life is dependent on various aspects of employee's work life. The first and the most important among them is economic aspect. The second important aspect is employment conditions. This order can be compared to Maslow's hierarchy of work motivation. Abraham Maslow arranged a person's motivational needs in a hierarchal manner. He believed that once a given level of need is satisfied, the next higher level of need has to be activated in order to motivate the individual.[1] In physiological needs again which are explained as basic and primary needs of employee by Maslow, once the employe is satisfied with the monetary benefits, he aspires for higher level of needs to be fulfilled i.e., good working/employment conditions.

However, this hierarchical local need not be in the same way. Sometimes, higher order needs may emerge along with or prior to the lower level needs. This priority depends upon the requirements, culture and region where employee works. As such physical working conditions may sometimes come prior to monetary aspect in order of preference of employee.

Working conditions come under 'Hygiene factors' of Herzberg's two-factor theory of motivation.[2] As such, though they do not motivate an employee, non-existence of good conditions do dissatisfy them.

An employee normally spends 8 hours at his workplace which is significant part of the employee's time. Hence, providing good working conditions play an important role in reducing employee dissatisfaction about the job. An impressive building with good furniture and other facilities impress employee more than anything else.

Employment conditions play more important role in service-oriented organisations like banks. The employee here has to constantly deal with customers of varying types. As such lot of patience and good reasoning is required. With inadequate facilities available an employee gets tired soon and cannot concentrate on his work.

Employment Conditions in Andhra Bank

Andhra Bank doesn't maintain any separate accounts to record the expenditure that is spend towards physical working conditions. This expenditure comes under general expenditure. As such exact figure of how much is spent on physical working conditions could not be derived at. But from informal discussions with the members of management, it is found that they spend considerable amount i.e., nearly twenty percent of the total expenditure towards maintenance of physical working conditions. They also expressed that most of this amount is spent to arrange facilities at new branches and to repair the old ones.

The process of restructuring furniture and other infrastructure facilities are not taken up by the management of the bank unless and until there are breakages to furniture. While constructing and furnishing new branches of the bank previous experiences are taken into consideration.

Some of the most important employment conditions are taken and the responses are recorded again mostly with the help of 5 point scale. 5 values are assigned to the 5 point scale and net values are ascertained. The analysis of these aspects in Andhra Bank and Vysya Bank is presented with the help of tables as and when required.

Management Views :

The management of Andhra Bank felt that the duration of rest they provide to employees is sufficient to some extent. The ascertained value is 0.60. The rest period that is provided to the employees is usually 1 hour to 1 hour 30 minutes. This rest is provided at lunch time. This is called "lunch hour". If they take half-an-hour to forty five minute to dine they have another half-an-hour to relax.

Andhra Bank Management's opinions on physical working condition presented in Table 5.1. Management respondents of Andhra Bank felt that the physical working conditions available to the employees are satisfactory. Majority of them expressed the opinion that they are either most positive or positive. They are positive to the extent of almost +1 (0.95).

Table 5.1 : Andhra Bank Management's Views on Safe and Healthy Working Conditions

Views of Management on Working Conditions	*Weighted Average Value*
Adequacy of Physical Working Conditions	0.60
Adequacy of Rent provided to employees	0.95

Source : Primary Data.

Employee's Views :

As far the feelings after day's work is concerned, majority of employees felt that they are neither tired not relaxed. But 57 of them felt that they are tired. But none of them either most positive (relaxed and very active) or most negative (very tired). The employees after their 7 hours workday with 1 hour 30 minutes to relax are neither tired nor relaxed. Provided they start their work day actively, they are tired to the extent of losing their activeness and not beyond that.

Regarding adequacy of physical working conditions, employees expressed varying views. Majority of employees expressed positive opinion when asked about good and clean drinking water facility. As many as 195 respondents out of 236 felt most positive, positive or not either positive or negative.

Canteen facilities are not available at any branch of the bank. Management does not provide any canteen facilities to its employees. Understandably the net ascertained value is –1.40.

Medical facility is another aspect which has drawn maximum negative attitude from employees. While there were none who felt most positive or neutral, 216 respondents out of 236 were either negative or most negative.

Transportation facility is also not available, according to the employees. They were collectively negative towards this aspect to the extent of –0.60 which is more than 50%.

Many of eminent sports persons are employees of Andhra Bank. In spite of this, the employees felt that sports and games facility is not good. Majority of them i.e., 194 respondents gave negative reply.

Library facility is another physical facility which is more important where most of the employees are educated. It is also important in such organisations where training should be provided to employees. Andhra Bank employees are negative regarding this facility to the extent of –0.54.

Apart from having rest period provided, employees should also have facilities for spending such rest period. To spend their rest period (lunch hour) they need to have some infrastructure facilities such as such room. Regarding this facility, the employees were negative to the extent of –0.99.

Air cooler or Air conditioner is another physical condition which gains more importance in hot places like Rayalaseema in Andhra Pradesh. During summer it is hard to spent 7-8 hours dealing with customers without cooling facility. Here majority employees of Andhra Bank i.e. 167 of 236 felt most negatively expressing that air coolers or air conditioners are absolutely not available.

Employee's view regarding physical working conditions are summarized in Table 5.2. Adequacy of rest duration is the last employment condition which was asked. Employees did not differ much from their earlier views regarding other conditions. Here again the net ascertained value is –0.70. Most of the employees were neutral when they were asked about how they felt after day's work. When directly asked about adequacy of rest duration they were clearly negative.

Trade union members were asked about their views regarding physical working conditions. They expressed opinions similar to those of employees. Majority of them felt negative regarding

Table 5.2 : Andhra Bank Employees Views on Physical Working Conditions

Views of Employees on Working Conditions	*Weighted Average Value*
Feelings after day's work	+ 0.07
Drinking water facilities	+ 0.20
Canteen facilities	– 1.40
Medical facilities	– 0.71
Transport facilities	– 0.66
Sports and Games facilities	– 0.43
Library facilities	– 0.54
Lunch room facilities	– 0.99
Air cooler/Air conditioner facilities	– 1.40
Adequacy of rest duration	– 0.70

Source : Primary Data.

physical facilities. Only few of them were neutral and none of them were positive. They also expressed that they can solve this problem through negotiations. As such trade unions are not satisfied with the employment conditions available but confident that this situation can be rectified through negotiations. Interestingly this aspect was not a serious issue ever negotiated with management.

Employment condition is an aspect where there is a difference of opinion among management, employees and trade unions. The management respondents of Andhra Bank were positive regarding physical conditions that are available to the employees. Employees and trade unions on the other hand are quite negative. Except drinking water facility where they were positive to the extent of 0.20, regarding all other facilities they are negative.

Unlike the case of monetary benefits where they shared similar views, in case of employment conditions they differed each other. On an average the employees of Andhra Bank expressed negative view regarding employment conditions to an extent of -0.73.

Employment Conditions in Vysya Bank

Vysya Bank also does not maintain any separate account for

expenditure on physical facilities. Similar to Andhra Bank they add this expenditure to general expenditure account. As such exact amount spent on this could not be derived at, management however felt that around 20% of the total amount is being spent on physical working conditions. This includes the amount spent on furnishing new branches. Management is providing facilities like water coolers at urban branches. Managements do not provide library facilities at the branch level. At some branches employees formed into informal clubs and are buying books and organising sports and games.

Questionnaires were distributed to the representatives of management, employees and trade unions from which their opinions are recorded. These opinions are presented in Table 5.3 and 5.4.

Table 5.3 : Vysya Bank Management's Opinion about Safe & Healthy Working Conditions

Views of Management on Working Conditions	*Weighted Average Value*
Adequacy of Physical Working Conditions	0.70
Adequacy of Rest provided to employees	1.14

Source : Primary Data.

Table 5.4 : Vysya Bank Employees Opinion on Physical Working Conditions

Views of Employees on Working Conditions	*Weighted Average Value*
Feelings after day's work	– 0.02
Drinking water facilities	0.10
Canteen facilities	– 1.38
Medical facilities	– 0.46
Transport facilities	– 1.40
Sports and Games facilities	– 1.81
Library facilities	– 1.43
Lunch room facilities	– 1.15
Air cooler/Air conditioner facilities	– 1.81
Adequacy of rest duration	– 0.29

Source : Primary Data.

Management's Attitudes

Regarding duration of rest provided to the employees, all seven representatives of management felt that the duration is sufficient for the employees to relax.

Management of Vysya Bank is quite satisfied with the duration of rest provided to the employees. Majority of employe's representatives on the other hand felt that they are tired.

Physical working condition is another aspect where the management and employees of Vysya Bank differs from each other. Management is positive with regard to the employment conditions, the weighted average being +0.70. Though not absolutely positive, they are collectively positive to the extent of 70%.

Employee's Attitudes

It is observed that the duration of rest provided to the employees is 1 hour to 1 hour and 15 minutes for lunch.

After 1 hour 15 minutes, of lunch hour majority of employees felt that they are tired after work hours. 70 out of 113 sample employees said they are tired.

Opinions of employees are also recorded regarding each of important physical working conditions. Drinking water facility is the only aspect where the employees are atleast neutral if not positive. Employees are negative regarding all other aspects of employment conditions. Weighted average value ascertained here is 0.10 which is close to neutral value of 0.

Regarding canteen facility, employees are clearly negative. 35 representatives out of 64 gave their negative attitude regarding canteen facility. Incidentally it is found out that the management of Vysya Bank do not provide any canteen facility at branches.

Medical facility is another condition where employees are negative to some extent. The weighted average value here is -0.40. Employees have sick leave and 'Medical Reimbursement'. But they do not have health centre or clinic facility available.

Transport facility comes first in the order of preference in case of employees at urban and suburban branches. 45 out of 64 employes are absolutely negative towards this facility expressing their grave dissatisfaction.

Sports and games is another facility where employees are more negative than in case of transport facility. The weighted average value here is –1.81, which is close to –2 (absolute negative value).

The employees are also devoid of library facility. Again 40 employees out of 64 are negative as far as library facility is concerned. But some of the employees felt that management encourages those who appear for examinations by way of giving free coaching.

Lunch room is another facility which is not available to the employees at branches. As such the weighted average value drawn here is –1.15.

Air cooler/Air conditioner facility is also not available to the employees. Ceiling fans are available at all branches. The is another facility where 46 out of 64 employees expressed their dissatisfaction.

Regarding adequacy of rest 35 employees out of 64 expressed their dissatisfaction. But interestingly, there are also 18 employees who are most satisfied with the available rest period. However the weighted average value is towards negative to some extent –0.29.

Representatives of trade unions generally are dissatisfied with the available working conditions. They felt that though management is providing minimum/basic facilities like drinking water facility, lighting, fans etc., changing needs of employees are not taken into consideration. For example, water coolers are not arranged. Instead, steel drums and earthen pots at some rural branches are only arranged.

Though the trade unions are dissatisfied with the available working conditions, they felt that this situation can be improved through negotiations. They are also considerate to take management's ability into account while demanding for more or improved facilities. For example, one of the representatives said that though ceiling fans cannot provide required cooling at hot places of Karnataka and Andhra, they cannot put pressure on management for air coolers/conditioners as it is beyond the ability of management to provide such luxuries at all branches of the bank.

Physical working conditions play a very important role in employee's work life in banking industry, where bank branches operate in rural and backward areas. With insufficient or improper physical conditions, it becomes all the more difficult for the employees to carry on their work for 7–8 hours. Bank is a service organisation. Customer's welfare is motto of banks. Dealing with varying types of customers all the day without proper facilities is almost impossible. As such working conditions in banks play a very important role.

Minimum facilities like good furniture like chairs, table cash counters and a separate grilled counter for cashier are provided by both the banks at all branches. Telephone facility is also provided to all branches except a very few rural branches where telephone connections are not available.

Andhra Bank is now insisting on having their own buildings even at rural place according to their specifications. So that they can have good facilities and spacious furniture arranged for employees.

However, Vysya Bank is still mostly dependent on rented premises. At Regional/Zonal level, they have their own premises.

Apart from all these facilities, management, employees and trade unions are enquired about other facilities which might seem minor from outset but cause dissatisfaction in absence. From the opinions gathered, interesting insights are developed.

Rest duration provided to the employees of Andhra Bank is 1 hour and 30 minutes. Management is mostly satisfied to the extent of 60% with the duration they provide. This duration is provided at mid-afternoon, mainly for lunch, Management is of the opinion that with one and half hours break in a 7 hours work day employee can sufficiently relax.

Employees of Andhra Bank on the other hand, expressed negative views towards the duration of rest to the extent of 70%. But regarding their relaxation after day's work is concerned, they are neither positive nor negative. Though duration of rest is not sufficient according to the employees, still they do not say that they are tired. It can be drawn here that the duration of rest is not insufficient to the extent of them getting tired after day's work.

Some of the employees also felt during informal chats that the rest provided during lunch time is sufficient. But they needed break in between starting of the day and lunch break. Though they can take coffee break for 10-15 minutes informally, they cannot usually come out of their counters till lunch break with heavy flow of customers. Many employees are often seen having beverages at their seats in the middle of their work. As such employees suggested to have a 15 minute break for tea at 11.00 A.M.

In case of Vysya Bank, management is again satisfied with the period of rest provided to the employees. They gave a positive +1 as their counterparts in Andhra Bank where they have given a value which is little less 0.60.

Employees of Vysya Bank gave their negative attitude towards the duration of rest. They also felt that they are tired after day's work with the given rest period. The employees of Vysya Bank are negative towards the rest duration and also say that they are tired whereas in case of Andhra Bank though employees are quite negative towards the duration of rest, they are neutral regarding their tiredness. It may be attributed to the fact that it is not only rest by which the employees relax, it is also through other physical facilities. Interesting job can be another factor which reduces tiredness of employees.

Other physical working conditions, like water, canteen, medical and library etc., have drawn positive attitude from managements of both the banks and negative attitude from the employees of both the banks. Both the managements are not absolutely positive, whereas the employees of Andhra Bank and Vysya Bank are negative to the extent of –0.73 and –1.07 respectively. It is observed that employees of Vysya Bank are more negative in their attitude towards physical working conditions than employees of Vysya Bank. As far as managements are concerned, management of Andhra bank is less positive than the management of Vysya Bank to the extent of 0.10.

The aspects which have drawn most negative view in case of both the banks are air cooler/air conditioner facility. Apart from this aspect, employees of Andhra Bank are also most negative towards canteen facility and employees of Vysya Bank are most negative towards games and sports facility.

As the rest duration is only at lunch time, if the employees need snacks or beverages in between, they have to have them within 10–15 minutes available during their busy work hours. As such they need cafeteria which is nearer to them. As no canteen facility is available to the employees, they are dissatisfied with this facility.

It is interesting to find out that the employees of Vysya Bank are most negative towards sports and games facility, though they are also negative towards other facilities.

Regarding air conditioner/air cooler, employees of both the banks are most dissatisfied. Intensity of scorching sun may be the reason for this. But the ability of management has to be taken into consideration to provide such costly facilities.

The employees of Andhra Bank are least negative towards sports and games facility. Many employees rated this facility as last in the order of preference of employees. The employees of Vysya Bank are least negative towards, rest duration provided to them.

The management of the banks may examine the possibilities of providing some of the facilities which not beyond their financial capabilities like lunch room facility. Transportation can be provided by way of vanpooling, where employees share the expenditure of a vehicle which is provided by the management. They can also encourage their employees to participate in games and sports.

The management of the banks are probably not aware of the dissatisfaction of employees towards working conditions. They are positive regarding the facilities provided to employees. Management also might have thought that working conditions are only drinking water, lighting, furniture accommodating employees etc. Thus it is suggested that the importance of other facilities also should be realised by management and put in efforts to provide them to employees taking their financial capabilities into consideration.

Notes:

1. Fred Luthans 'Organisational Behaviour', Mc. Graw-Hill.
2. Fred Luthans *op. cit.*, p. 243.

6

Social Aspects of Quality of Work Life

Introduction

Social system plays an important role in the work life of an employee. Social system is a complex set of human relationships interacting in many ways. Possible interactions are as limitless as stars in the universe. Within a single organisation, the social system includes all the people in it and their relationships to each other and to the outside world.[1]

The social system affects an employee's work life. Social and work life of an employee are interdependent. For example, the work/job of an employee specifies his social peers. Since most of the employees are migrated to their work place, it is their colleagues and work-related people with whom they socialise. Social group of employees is formed based mostly upon their job.

An employee plays many roles at his work place and in a social system. An employee plays roles of subordinate, boss, trade union member, secretary to a cultural club, a husband and a father. All these roles interact and influence his work life. An employee can lead a qualitative work life if all these roles correlate and interact positively. As such social aspects play a very important role in 'Quality of Work Life'.

'Social aspect influence 'Quality of Work Life' in many ways. One is social integration within the bank. Social integration is social/interpersonal relations that employees share at work place with his superiors and subordinates. If he has strained relations with his boss, his work life is invariably affected. The opportunity for socialisation with colleagues is an important aspect of 'Quality of Work Life'.

Another social aspect is social relevance of job. The social status that he enjoys outside, the respect his job commands in his social groups affect his work life.

Another part of social aspect is other institutions like family, trade unions and other informal groups of which the employee is a member.

The demands of the family of an employee and that of trade unions affect the work life of that employee tremendously. If the family of an employee demands more and more of his time he cannot put in effective work, and vice versa. As such positive co-ordination between his roles in the organisation and home and trade unions is a requirement for effective 'Quality of Work Life'.

Constitutionalism is another important social aspect which an employee seeks for in his organisation. Basically constitutionalism is that all employees should be treated fairly and justly as humans without discrimination. Basic rights of an employee like protecting his privacy, giving him chance to present his view, whenever a conflict arises, etc. should be protected.

Banking is an industry which gains a lot of respect and goodwill in the society. As such a bank employee always attracts attention and importance. This recognition gives confidence and morale to the employees to put in hard work and sincerity into his job.

Andhra Bank has been almost synonym for the word 'bank' for many years. This explains its status and image in public. A job with Andhra Bank is much envied. This image of Andhra Bank is morale-boosting for its employees. Andhra Bank is also one of the oldest banks with large number of employees on its payrolls. As such, the employees have a feeling of belonging to a big group.

Efforts are made at Andhra Bank to maintain constitutionalism to maintain good interpersonal relations in the bank.

Vysya Bank, though comparatively younger, is boasting of its comradery among its employees. Vysya Bank always emphasises team work[2] which provides a sense of belongingness to the employees. With an employee strength of 4,314, the operations of Vysya Bank are quite integrated and the bank is like a closely-knit family.

Vysya Bank is also putting in its efforts to have a good constitutionalism. Constitutionalism is the backbone of good interpersonal relations. But there are very few cases which needed any strong action against any employee.[3]

Andhra Bank and Vysya Bank differ from each other in three ways. The first one is Andhra Bank is in public sector and Vysya Bank in private sector. The second difference is Andhra Bank is one of the oldest banks being incorporated in 1923, during the struggle for independence and has struggled to withstand various political and economic calamities of the nation. Whereas Vysya Bank is comparatively younger and incorporated in fairly good economic and political conditions. The third difference between these two banks is that Andhra bank consists of a large number of employees i.e., 15,604. As such there is a wide network of communication, As against this, Vysya bank is operating with only 4,314 employees. As a result, communication here is quick and direct. As a result, employees have a feeling that they are part of whatever goes on in the Bank.

With these main characters and differences between the two banks, at attempt is made to evaluate the feelings of employees regarding social integration and social relevance of work, and its effect on 'Quality of Work Life'.

Social Integration

Andhra Bank Managements Views

The managements of both the banks are enquired about whether good interpersonal relations exist in the bank as part of social integration. The management of Andhra Bank is positive in this aspect to an extent of 0.35. So, the management is only 35 per cent positive with regard to the good inter-personal relations. Management opinions are summarised in Table 6.1

Employees Views

It is very interesting to note that, the employees of Andhra Bank in spite of management, are quite positive regarding the state

Table 6.1 : Andhra Bank Management's Opinion on Interpersonal Relations

Opinion of Management on Interpersonal Relations	*Weighted Average Value*
Existence of good Inter-personal Relations	0.35

Source : Primary Data.

of interpersonal relations that are existing in the bank. They gave positive value i.e., +0.92 to this aspect.

The trade union members of the bank are also positive in general regarding interpersonal relations that are existing in the bank.

Apart from this aspect many other issues are enquired with employees as part of social relevance and social integration which are summarised in Table 6.2. In social integration the employees are asked about leadership style of their superior. Around 70 per cent of the employees stated the leadership-style to be democratic. A few of them i.e., around 5 per cent felt it to be paternalistic.

Regarding their colleagues around 9 per cent of them felt that they like and respect their colleagues. Only 8 per cent of them said that they are indifferent to their colleagues.

Table 6.2 : Andhra Bank Employees Opinion about Social Integration

Prospects of Social Integration	*Weighted Average Value*
Possibility to mingle and chat with colleagues	0.08
Expectations of Boss	0.67
Existence of Interpersonal Relations	0.92
Consolation about matters concerning employees	1.20
Free atmosphere to give suggestions	0.87
Acceptance of suggestions	0.77
Interference of boss	0.22
Co-operation from subordinates	1.39

Source : Primary Data.

Chance to mingle and that with colleagues is almost non-existent in the bank. The employes gave an average value which is close to zero i.e., +0.08

Employees also feel that their boss expects something more from them than what they can contribute, with 144 out of a sample of 236 either strongly agree or agree.

Employes are always consulted regarding any matter which concerns them. During work, whenever they are involved, they are consulted. Employees are more than positive regarding this aspect with ratings of +1.20.

Good interpersonal relations reflects in the way superiors and subordinates carry on work with each others suggestions. Andhra Bank employees are almost positive in this aspect also. They are close to positive value +1, i.e., 0.87. Employees feel free to come out and suggest anything to their superiors to an extent to 87 per cent.

Interpersonal relations also depends upon how the suggestions are received. Even though employees are free to give suggestions and they are encouraged in this regard, if these suggestions are never accepted or mocked at, relations are strained. But here again, employees are positive to an extent of 77 per cent. 77 per cent of their suggestions are accepted with fine hands.

The employees responded negatively when asked about the interference of boss in their work. The weighted average value here is –0.22. So, evidently boss does not unnecessarily interfere with the work of employees.

They were also very cordial and positive regarding cooperation from their subordinates. While 201 employees are either very positive or positive, there were few who responded negatively. This can be viewed as the reflection of good interpersonal relations.

The trade union members are generally satisfied and positive as far as social integration is concerned. They had problem with management only regarding transfer policy. For all problems the means is negotiations. They also felt that in general good interpersonal relations exist in the bank resulting in social integration.

All three parties of bank i.e., the management, employees and trade union members are satisfied with the social integration of the bank. While management is satisfied to an extent of 0.22 employees are almost fully satisfied. Trade Union members also are fully satisfied with their relations with employees and management.

Especially regarding certain important aspects where an element of ego exists like consulting employees about matters which concerns them, suggestions being accepted by superiors, cooperation from subordinate employees are fully satisfied. This is a remarkable achievement by bank in this regard.

Opinions of Management of Vysya Bank

The management of Vysya Bank is little more positive than their counterparts in Andhra Bank. Regarding the existence of good interpersonal relations in the bank, they gave a weighted average value of +0.42. Their opinion is summarised in Table 6.3.

Table 6.3 : Vysya Bank Management's Opinion on Interpersonal Relations

Opinion of Management of Vysya Bank on Interpersonal Relations	*Weighted Average Value*
Existence of good Inter-personal Relations	0.42

Source : Primary Data.

Views of Employees of Vysya Bank

Employees of Vysya Bank are little more positive in this aspect than management. They rated this aspect as +0.65. The opinion of employees are summarised in Table 6.4.

The style of leadership in the bank is democratic, according to the employees. But some of the employees felt that though the policy of the bank is democratic, leadership-style basically depends upon the nature and ego of each individual. In an informal chat they expressed that some of their bosses are autocrats.

Like their counterparts in Andhra Bank, employees of Vysya Bank also felt that they respect and like their colleagues. None of them expressed any negative attitude towards their colleagues.

As far as opportunity to mingle with colleagues and chat, 35 out of 68 employees are either fully satisfied or satisfied. As such

Table 6.4 : Vysya Bank Employees Opinion about Social Integration

Opinion of Employees About Social Integration	*Weighted Average Value*
Possibility to mingle and chat with colleagues	0.51
Expectations of boss	1.28
Existence of interpersonal relations	0.65
Consolation about matters concerning employees	0.48
Free atmosphere to give suggestions	0.84
Acceptance of suggestions	0.09
Interference of Boss	0.75
Co-operation from subordinates	1.00

Source : Primary Data.

they are satisfied to an extent of 50 per cent.

Regarding expectation of boss, employees strongly feel that, the boss expects more than what they can contribute. The weighted average value they gave here is +1.28.

Employees of Vysya Bank are satisfied to an extent of 50 per cent regarding their being consulted about matter which concerns them. 38 employees out of 64 are either fully satisfied or satisfied regarding this aspect.

They are almost perfectly satisfied regarding their feelings to give suggestions. The weighted average value they gave here is 0.84 which is close to +1. But they are not as positive regarding their suggestions being accepted. Here they are positive only to an extent of +0.09.

Vysya Bank employees felt that their boss interferes with their work more than what he is supposed to unlike employees of Andhra Bank who were negative to this aspect, 48 employees out of 64 were positive regarding this aspect.

Though employees share negative attitude towards their superior, they are satisfied with the co-operation they receive from their subordinates. They gave an average value of +1 here.

Members of trade unions of Vysya Bank are positive towards the aspect of interpersonal relations and resulting social integration in the bank. They expressed that good cooperation and contacts exist between management and employees. In fact, management is trying to put the employees at ease. They also expressed that though some of the managers are autocratic in their leadership-style, no one is generally against any employee.

On the whole, the management of Vysya Bank is more positive towards social integration in the bank. They are more positive than management of Andhra Bank to an extent of 0.10. An interesting phenomena is, though management of Andhra Bank is less satisfied with inter-personal relations in the organisation, employees are quite satisfied. Andhra Bank employees are fully satisfied with the existing inter-personal relations in the organisation in spite of management which though positive, is satisfied only to some extent.

The employees of Vysya Bank on the other hand are more satisfied than management regarding this aspect. They are satisfied to an extent of around 70 per cent.

In case of other important aspects such as consulting employees regarding matters that concerns them, unnecessary interferences of boss, opportunity to give suggestions, employees of Andhra Bank are most satisfied whereas employees of Vysya Bank though on positive side are not that satisfied.

Members of trade unions of both the banks are generally satisfied with existing inter-personal relations in the bank and resulting social integration.

Social Relevance of Work

Another part of social integration is social relevance of work. The societal image and respect that employees work command influences his quality of work life. The job also in turn affects his societal status and peer-circle. The weighted average value drawn here is 1.29. A bank employee always drawn dignity and respect in the society.

The employees are also positive regarding what they can talk about their job outside their work place. As many as 190 employees of total sample expressed that they can proudly talk about their job outside the work place.

A challenging job motivates an employee and influences his

Table 6.5 : Andhra Bank Employees Opinion on Social Relevance of Work

Employees Opinion on Aspects of Social Relevance of Work	*Weighted Average Value*
Usefulness of work	0.99
Reaction of friends and relations	0.55
Improvement of social status with job	–0.29
Reference of job outside	0.57
Dignity and respect of job	1.29
Challenging job	0.25

Source : Primary Data.

Table 6.6 : Vysya Bank Employees Opinion on Social Relevance of Work

Aspects of Social Relevance of Work	*Weighted Average Value*
Usefulness of work	1.18
Reaction of friends and relations	0.72
Improvement of social status with job	1.31
Reference of job outside	0.82
Dignity and respect of job	1.21
Challenging job	0.68

Source : Primary Data.

Quality of Work Life. Challenging job gives life to the work. Regarding this aspect, the employees are positive to an extent of 0.25.

On the whole, the employees of Andhra Bank are positive regarding relevance of their work except the aspect of their relatives reaction towards their job.

Views of Vysya Bank Employees

The employees of Vysya Bank are also generally positive towards the social relevance of their job. It is interesting to note that none of the sample employees have given a negative opinion to any of the queries regarding social relevance of work.

The employees are more than positive regarding their putting in useful work to the society. Because the very nature of their business is service to the society, understandably they are more than positive. The weighted average value here is 1.18.

Reactions of relatives towards their job is also positive according to the Vysya Bank employees. Forty-six employees out of a sample of 64 agreed that their relatives react enviously to their job.

Regarding improvement in social status because of their job in the bank also, the employees are more than positive. The weighted average value drawn here is 1.31.

Around 80 per cent of them feel proud of talking about their job outside workplace. Fifty five of the total sample agreed to this statement that they feel proud of talking about their job outside work place/bank.

Job providing sense of dignity and respect again has drawn a more than positive value. The net weighted average value here is +1.21.

According to the employees of Vysya Bank their job is challenging one to an extent of +0.68. They are more positive in this regard than their counterparts in Andhra Bank.

On an average, the employees of Andhra Bank are satisfied with the positive image of their job with the bank or the social relevance of their job to an extent of 0.63, whereas the employees of Vysya Bank are positive to an extent of 0.98. Though both the groups are positive the Vysya Bank employees are more positive.

It can be concluded that the employees of Vysya Bank believe that their Bank holds a good image in the public than Andhra Bank. This is a very morale-boasting phenomena. But as far as existence of social integration in the Bank is concerned, the employees of Andhra bank are more satisfied than that of Vysya Bank though both are generally on positive side.

On an average, the employees of Andhra Bank are positive to an extent of 0.76, whereas Vysya Bank employees are positive to the extent of 0.51. In fact, the employees of Andhra Bank are positive in this regard in spite of the management which is not so positive.

Balance Between Family and Work Life

Apart from social relevance and social integration another important social aspect of employees work life is his family and trade unions. The family life plays an important role in the work life of employee. Family is a social institution which has the greatest influence on the behaviour of employee. His family background is bound to affect his work life. Indians by nature give priority to domestic-life than work-life. The intimacy among family members is much required in our culture. This in turn demands much of employees time and attention. Another important aspect of family life is that the husband/father has to take care of many chores such as dropping the children at school, bringing them back and most of the shopping etc. The wife/mother is still mostly confined to home in India. As such the employee develops mental stress. From the profiles of employees it is found out that ninety per cent of employees are married. sixty per cent of employees who fall within the age group of less than 30 years are married. As such the family responsibilities start right from the beginning of his career.

The demands of family on female employee are more. The sample contains only two per cent of female employees. She has to attend children and other domestic chores. We come across rushing working women in buses and roads. Their quality of work life invariably gets affected due to their mental tensions that they experience at home.

As such balance between family and work life is very important. Effort is made to find out the extent of this balance in both the banks through questionnaires. Among three parties, employees are the only party which was enquired about family-life, as they are the best judges of their experience. Their feelings are sum-

Table 6.7 : Opinions of Employees regarding Balance between their Family and Work Life

Aspects of balance between family and work life	*Weighted Average Value*
Thinking of work at home	0.06
Carrying work to home	– 1.30

Source : Primary Data.

marised in Table 6.7.

Opinion of Employees of Andhra Bank

Sleeping time apart majority of the employees of Andhra Bank i.e. 157 felt that they spend around 6-8 hours with their family, 65 of them expressed that they spend 8-10 hours. And 14 employees spend only 4-6 hours with their family. Incidentally all these 14 employees are active members of trade unions.

One hundred and ninety eight employees of the total sample of 236 felt negatively regarding their spouses' feeling that they cannot stand to the expectation of family because of their job. Rest of them are either unmarried or positive about their spouses feeling that they could not stand to the expectations. Interestingly, this group does not include any female employee.

Most of the employees think of their work at home only now and then. Seventy five of the total sample fall into this category. As such weighted average value here is +0.06.

Almost none of the employees carry their work home. Weighed average value ascertained here is -1.30. The nature of work at banks is mostly confidential and employees are usually not allowed to carry their work home. So, this aspect does not disturb their family life.

On the whole, it can be concluded that the employees of Andhra Bank have a good balance between their family and work-life only with few exceptions.

Opinions of Employees of Vysya Bank

As far as employees of Vysya Bank are concerned, they are not as positive as employees of Andhra Bank though generally they are either positive or neutral. Their opinions regarding balance between family and work life are presented in Table 6.8.

Table 6.8 : Opinions of Employees of Vysya Bank regarding Balance Between Their Family and Work Life

Aspects of balance between Family and Work Life	*Weighted Average Value*
Thinking of work at home	0.26
Carrying work to home	– 1.29

Source : Primary Data.

Only two of the total sample of 64 felt that they spend only 4-6 hours with their family. A majority of 52 expressed that they spend 6-8 hours at home.

In case of employees of Vysya Bank, complaints from spouses of employees are more than that of employees of Andhra Bank. Thirty seven employees out of 64 expressed that they face complaints from their spouses that they cannot stand expectations of family due to their job. Rest of them are either not married or positive.

The employees are positive to the extent of +0.26 that they think of their work at home.

Regarding carrying work-home, employees of Vysya Bank are also quite negative. As said earlier, a bank employee cannot carry his work home.

On the whole, the employees of both the banks are generally satisfied with the balance between their dual roles. Andhra Bank employees seem to be more positive.

Regarding the time that they spend at home, employees of both the banks mostly felt it as 6–8 hours which is fair. Six-eight hours of time can be shared fairly between children, spouse and other domestic chores.

Expectations of spouses of Vysya Bank employees are usually not met. Little more than half of the employees of Vysya Bank are dissatisfied with the attitude of their spouses. This dissatisfaction affects their 'Quality of Work Life' to that extent.

Thinking of work at home is more in case of employees of Vysya Bank. However, this cannot be put as a negative dimension, unless employees are so preoccupied with this thought process that they cannot enjoy their family life, though they spend much time. Otherwise thinking of one's work at home is quite common.

Regarding bringing work home, both the groups of employees are negative. Since the nature of bank's job is such that the employees are not allowed to take their work home, employees of both the banks are equally negative.

On the whole, except for meeting the expectations of spouses of employees, the employees of both the banks feel that there is a balance between their family and work life.

Balance Between Trade Unions and Work Life

Trade Unions are an important part of the social aspects in an employee's work life. This is the case especially with bank employees as almost all of them are part of one union or the other. The relations of employees with trade unions, and their relations with management through trade unions are all the factors which affect the work life of employees. As such effort is made to assess the effect of trade unions on quality of work life.

Opinions of management and employees are collected regarding functioning of trade unions and their efforts to improve 'Quality of Work Life'. The opinions of managements of Andhra Bank and Vysya Bank and that of the employees of Andhra Bank and Vysya Bank are summarised in Tables 6.9, 6.10 and 6.11, 6.12 respectively. A separate questionnaire is also distributed to the sample of trade union members to assess their opinions.

Andhra Bank Management's Point of View

The Management of Andhra Bank felt that the effort of trade union towards increasing pay of employees to improve 'Quality of Work Life' is around 50 per cent. The weighted average assessed here is +0.57. As such trade unions do work towards improving the pay-scales of employees to improve their 'Quality of Work Life'.

Management of Andhra Bank felt that improvement of safe and healthy working conditions is also the aim of trade unions, but the extent of effort is not as much as in case of improving pay-scales of employees. The weighted average value assessed here is 0.35.

Table 6.9 : Andhra Bank Management's Opinion regarding Efforts of Union in Improving Quality of Work Life

Efforts of Union in Improving QWL	*Weighted Average Value*
Adequate and fiar pay	0.57
Safe and healthy working conditions	0.35
Participative management	–0.32
Career planning and growth	–0.23
Interpersonal relations	0.22

Source : Primary Data.

Regarding practicing participative style of management and improvement of career-planning and growth, the management is negative to the extent of -0.32 and 0.23 respectively. As such it can be drawn that the Trade Unions of Andhra Bank do not concern themselves regarding career growth or participative management.

The positive contacts between management and employees are evident from the opinion of management of Andhra Bank that Trade Unions do put in efforts to improve interpersonal relations in the bank. A majority of 54 of total sample are neutral and 37 of them are positive.

Andhra Bank Employees Point of View

Most of sample employees chosen from Andhra Bank are all members of Trade Unions. Their opinions regarding improvement of 'Quality of Work Life' through improving pay scales, working-conditions etc., coincides with the opinions of management of the bank.

Regarding improvement in pay-scales and safe and healthy working conditions, the employees are positive to the extent of more than 50 per cent. The weighted average values are 0.70 and 0.55 respectively.

Developing human capabilities for career advancement has drawn a negative value of -0.18. The effort of trade unions by way of arranging seminars and lectures etc., was assessed. Because in an institution like bank, improvement of human capabilities is what helps in career advancement.

Table 6.10 : Andhra Bank Employees' Opinion regarding Efforts of Union in Improving Quality of Work Life

Efforts of Union in Improving QWL	*Weighted Average Value*
Adequate and fiar pay	0.70
Safe and healthy working conditions	0.28
Participative management	-0.18
Career planning and growth	0.14
Interpersonal relations	0.04

Source: Primary Data.

Table 6.11 : Vysya Bank Management's Opinion regarding Efforts of Union in Improving Quality of Work Life

Efforts of Union in Improving QWL	*Weighted Average Value*
Adequate and fiar pay	1.00
Safe and healthy working conditions	0.57
Participative management	0.70
Career planning and growth	0.14
Interpersonal relations	–0.28

Source : Primary Data.

Regarding establishing good inter-personal relations, trade unions are putting efforts to the extent of only 0.14, according to the employees of Andhra Bank.

Employees of Andhra Bank felt that trade unions did not concern themselves in the establishment of good conflict-resolution mechanism. This aspect yielded a negative weighted average value of -0.03.

Finally, regarding career-planning and development, employees are mostly neutral, though the weighted average value is little above neutral value i.e., 0.04. As all employees of chosen sample are members of trade unions. Their opinions are considered as the feelings of trade unions Also.

The management of Andhra Bank is positive regarding efforts of trade unions in improving monetary aspects of employees and working-conditions. However, they are negative towards Trade unions efforts towards improving practices.

Regarding career-planning and growth, though the management is positive, it is only little above neutral value 0. The weighted-average value here is 0.14.

However, establishment of inter-personal relations yielded mostly negative from management. Management is negative to the extent of -0.28 towards the efforts at Unions in establishing good inter-personal relations.

View Point of Employees of Vysya Bank

It is found that in the process of analysis that all employees of chosen sample from Vysya Bank are members of trade unions.

Their views regarding aspects of QWL and their efforts to improve them neither coincide with that of the management nor with that of their counterparts in Andhra Bank.

Table 6.12 : Vysya Bank Employees' Opinion regarding Efforts of Union in Improving Quality of Work Life

Efforts of Union in Improving QWL	*Weighted Average Value*
Adequate and flat pay	0.53
Good working conditions	0.68
Improvement of human capabilities	0.34
Interpersonal relations	0.34
Conflict resolution mechanism	0.00
Career planning and growth	0.46

Source : Primary Data.

The employees are positive to the extent of 0.53 and 0.68 regarding their efforts to improve monetary-benefits of employees and working-conditions respectively. Regarding development of human capabilities, establishing good inter-personal relations and career-planning and development, they are positive to the extent of 0.34, 0.34 and 0.46 respectively. However, establishing good conflict-resolution mechanism has yielded an absolute neutral value 0.

Among both the banks, management of Vysya Bank is more satisfied with the functioning of the unions in their bank. According to the management, unions of Vysya Bank are working towards establishing participative management, whereas in Andhra Bank, managers are negative to this aspect. As such the employes of Andhra Bank are either not aware of the significance of democratic-style of management or they already have it in the organisation. Inter-personal relations is another area where management differ. Here management of Andhra Bank is positive whereas that of Vysya bank is negative. Inter-personal relations is an important aspect of QWL that all parties have to work towards it. Management of Vysya Bank expresses lack of any efforts from the Union side which may be considered as a loophole. Importance of inter-personal relations should be realised by the employees and Unions of the organisation. Management also can put efforts to educate employees in this area.

The trade unions of Vysya Bank are working more towards improving various components of Quality of Work Life, according to the employees of those banks. The employees of Vysya Bank are positive while responding to the efforts of unions in improving various components of QWL, whereas Andhra bank employees responded negatively to the efforts of unions in improving human capabilities and conflict-resolution mechanism. Vysya Bank employees are positive to the extent of 0.34 towards human capabilities and neutral regarding conflict-resolution mechanism. As such it can be assumed that employees and unions are considering improvement of these aspects as the role responsibility of management. Management can make efforts to educate employees regarding the significance of those aspects and their role in improvement.

Unions of Andhra Bank are giving prime importance to the monetary aspects and second place to the working-conditions and vice-versa in case of Unions of Vysya Bank.

Employees also expressed that the unions of Andhra Bank do not work towards improvement of human capabilities whereas the union of Vysya Bank do work to the extent of 34 per cent. Improvement of human capabilities is an important aspect of QWL and also it leads to the improvement of many other aspects. Unions of Andhra Bank ought to realise the significance of this aspect. Unions also hod the responsibilities, such as improving human capabilities, by way of arranging lectures and seminars etc., apart from negotiating with the management regarding monetary-benefits and working-conditions.

Interestingly, the management of Vysya Bank is positive to the extent of 70 per cent regarding unions efforts in establishing participative management in the Bank, while Andhra bank management is negative to this aspect. High rating by Vysya Bank management shows good understanding and effort of unions in this direction.

But regarding unions maintaining inter-personal relations, management of Vysya Bank is negative. Maintenance of interpersonal relations is an important area of HRM to improve quality of work life. Management's disappointment regarding this aspect is most regrettable.

Union members of both the banks expressed that means of improving these components is mainly negotiations.

Constitutionalism in Bank

The last important social aspect is constitutionalism prevailing in the banks.

In Andhra Bank, there is conflict-resolution mechanism in the bank, which is strictly adhered to. There is a committee called 'Joint Consultative Committee' formed at zonal level, which takes up conflict resolution process.

The committee sends notices to both the parties and allows them to express their views. They also have talks with the parties if necessary, before arriving at a solution. The decision taken by the committee is to be abided by both the parties. Joint Consultative Committee is formed for officers cadre. For Award Staff there is a separate committee which is called 'Industrial Relations Committee' which is formed with the objective of maintaining good Industrial Relations in the bank.[4]

Grievance-handling is done at branch level. This process is done informally by branch manager. If any solution cannot be reached at branch level, the zonal regional manager takes up the issues and tries to solve. Only if he cannot reach at any solution the employee can represent his issue to central office. But usually issues are solved at branch level.[5]

Opinions of Andhra Bank Management

Management, employees and trade union members are asked about their views regarding constitutionalism in the bank and their views are recorded in Table 6.13 and 6.14.

Table 6.13 : Andhra Bank Management's Opinion on Constitutionalism in Bank

Management's Opinion on Constitutionalism	*Weighted Average Value*
Appropriations of conflict solution mechanism	–0.04

Source : Primary Data.

Management of Andhra Bank is mostly neutral regarding appropriateness of conflict-resolution mechanism. They are negative to some extent. The weighted-average value ascertained here is -0.04. As such the management is neither negative nor positive towards this aspect.

Opinions of Employees of Andhra Bank

Employees of Andhra Bank are positive to the extent of 0.10. Majority of employees i.e., 150 out of 236 employees are neutral regarding this aspect. They are also asked about their views regarding maintaining their privacy. Employees are positive regarding this aspect to the extent of 0.59. Their personal matters do not enter into their work-place in anyway. Only at the time of recruitment, they are asked to fill in their bio-data which covers their personal issues to some extent. Though these forms are with management, they do not use these forms to invade the privacy of the employees.

Table 6.14 : Andhra Bank Employees Opinion on Constitutionalism in Bank

Management's Opinion on Constitutionalism	*Weighted Average Value*
Privacy regarding personal matters	0.59
Appropriateness of conflict resolution mechanism	0.10

Source : Primary Data.

The members of trade unions also are generally satisfied with conflict-reduction mechanism in the bank. Still, they suggest that management should negotiate with trade unions to improve the conflict-reduction mechanism and grievances-handling.

The management, employees and members of trade unions of Vysya Bank are also asked similar questions as in Andhra Bank and their views are depicted in Table 6.15 and 6.16 respectively.

Vysya Bank Management about Constitutionalism

Almost all management respondents (i.e., 6 out of 7) of Vysya Bank are either positive or neutral regarding the conflict-reduction mechanism available in the bank. Here again conflicts are mostly resolved at branch level.

Table 6.15 : Vysya Bank Management's Opinion on Constitutionalism in Bank

Management's Opinion on Constitutionalism	*Weighted Average Value*
Appropriations of conflict solution mechanism	0.28

Source : Primary Data.

Employees Views

Employees of Vysya Bank on the other hand are negative though to a very little extent towards conflict-reduction mechanism. The weighted average value ascertained here is 0.03.

Table 6.14 : Vysya Bank Employees' Opinion on Constitutionalism in Bank

Employess' Opinion on Constitutionalism	*Weighted Average Value*
Privacy regarding personal matters	0.96
Appropriateness of conflict-resolution mechanism	–0.03

Source : Primary Data.

As far as maintaining privacy of employees personal matter is concerned, employees views are very close to positive +1 i.e., 0.96. The employees felt that their personal matters had nothing to do with their work at bank.

Trade union members are mostly contradicting each other regarding conflict-resolution mechanism. Some of them expressed their satisfaction, some of them felt that there is undue insistance from management to solve the conflict peacefully and not refer the matter to higher-levels. Then, justification is not done to the aggrieved parties, though their problems are serious and genuine.

Management of Vysya Bank is said to be striving hard at providing fair conflict-resolution mechanism and grievance procedure. When conflict between employees and employee and management at branch level, cannot be solved then the issue is finally carried on to corporate office. But it is only on rare occasions that any issue passes on to Corporate Office. At Branch and Divisional levels managers deal with the conflicts whereas at corporate-level industrial relations committee deals with the mechanism.

Grievance procedure is taken up by a committee which is an informal group consisting of Deputy General Manager, General Manager and Officer, Personnel). But minor issues are mostly encouraged to be solved at branch level informally.

Notes :

1. Keith Davis & John W. Newstrom, "*Human Behaviour at Work*", McGraw-Hill Book Company, New York, 1989.
2. *46th Annual Report*, Vysya Bank.
3. *Personnel Records*, Vysya Bank, Head Office, Bangalore.
4. *Personnel Records* of Andhra Bank, Hyderabad.
5. *Ibid.*

7

Human Resource Development Aspects of Quality of Work Life

An important phase of results of Quality of Work Life is Human Resources Development of existing employees. The physical improvement of QWL leads to the improvement of economic and employment conditions whereas improvement of social and psychological aspects of QWL provides conductive environment for development of human resources.

Economic and employment conditions are basic needs of employees to be satisfied. After fulfilment of these needs, employees looks forward for the fulfilment of social and psychological needs. Satisfaction of Social and Psychological needs of employee changes the behaviour of employees. The enhancement of employee's skills, capabilities and potentialities lead to the employee development and his job-satisfaction.

Human resource is the total sum of knowledge, skills creative abilities, talents, aptitudes values and beliefs.[1]

Abilities and talents play an important role in deciding the efficiency and effectiveness of an organisation's work-force. Enhancement of utilisation value of human resources depends on the improvement of human resource aspects like skills, knowledge, creative abilities and talents and moulding of other aspects like values, beliefs, aptitudes and attitudes to suit the changing needs of the organisation and employers.

Human Resources Development acquires all the more importance in service-organisations like Banks where human resource plays a crucial role. The creative-abilities, capabilities and knowledge of human resource are significant in case of service-organisations where the very nature of functioning needs all these qualities of employees.

The aspect of Human Resource Development also assumes importance in present day conditions where there is a severe competition among various organisations and as the spectrum of functions of organisation are widening. The Banks in particular are entering various innovative areas of service of their customers. This enlargement of jobs need enhancement of capabilities and potentialities of employees. Improved performance of Bank through enhance capabilities of its employees also leads to the improved social-image of bank. This in turn satisfies social needs of employees.

From the adopted criteria, to find out the opinions of employees about various aspects like opportunity to develop human capabilities through various means, career-planning and growth, work itself and others like organisation structure leads to the enhancement of capabilities and potentialities of human resource.

Employees are to be given a chance to develop their capabilities like skills and knowledge. Enhancement of capabilities leads to better performance on job. An attempt is made to find out the experience of both the banks in the development of human resources by means of opinions of management, employees and Trade Union members through questionnaires.

Andhra Bank has HR cells at Corporate and Regional levels, which work towards the improvement of HR of the employees.

Development of Human Capabilities

The capabilities of employees can be developed through utilising them properly while they are on the job and giving a chance for them to participate in the higher-levels of management. Opinions of managements of both Andhra Bank and Vysya Bank are collected in this regard.

Opinion of Management of Andhra Bank :

The management of Andhra Bank feels that they have given

an opportunity to develop human capabilities to an extent of 55% on an average. They responded to two aspects of development of human capabilities.

Management of Andhra Bank is positive to an extent of +0.61 regarding providing employees an opportunity to participate in management.

As far as utilisation of employee's potentialities on their job is concerned, management is 56% positive. As such management of Andhra Bank feels that they provide opportunity to employees to develop their capabilities to an extent of about 55%. Their opinions are summarised in Table 7.1.

Table 7.1 : Views of Andhra Bank Management on Utilization of Human Capabilites

Management's Views about the Utilization of Human Capabilities	*Weighted Average Value*
Opportunity to participate in management	0.61
Appropriate use of potentialities on job	0.56

Source : Primary Data

Opinion of the Employees of Andhra Banks :

The opinions of employees of Andhra Bank are also gathered with regard to development of human capabilities and quantified in Table 7.2.

Learning is the most important aspect of any job. Unless an employes has some thing new to learn on the job he will loose

Table 7.2 : Views of Andhra Bank Employees on Utilization of Human Capabilites

Employees' Views about the Utilization of Human Capabilities	*Weighted Average Value*
Opportunity to learn new skills on job	0.55
Job making use of existing skills	0.72
Consultation before any major decision	0.22
Encouragement to participate in management	0.06

Source : Primary Data

interest and motivation to continue his job efficiently. More than half of the employees of Andhra Bank are either most satisfied or satisfied in this regard. However since almost equal number of employees are also spread through other categories, the weighted-average value ascertained is +0.55.

Under-employment is a serious threat to Human Resource Development. Job should make use of all existing capabilities. Employee feels alienated if the job does not use his capabilities to a complete extent. Employees, however, are satisfied in this regard. The weighted average-value of employee's opinions is +0.72.

Democratic style of management also helps in the development of human capabilities of employees. Employee opinions are collected with regard to the level of consultation of management with employees before any major decision is taken. Employees through expressed positive view, are not much satisfied. As many as 60 out of 236 employees have expressed neutral views. The weighted average value of the views ascertained here is 0.22.

Another important style of management is participative management. Unless there is an encouragement from management in this regard there would be neither initiation nor commitment from employees. Employees are almost neutral regarding management's encouragement towards participative management.

The Union Members are also consulted regarding the existing situation in the Bank regarding development of human capabilities and their part in this aspect.

The Union members are generally satisfied with the opportunity given by management. Management conducts training and developmental programmes to improve their capabilities. Though Unions encourage their members to undergo training, they do not have any contribution to make to the management. Trade Unions view that, management consults all major Unions before taking any important decision, like enhancement of monetary-benefits, or any policy which effects employees in general.

Vysya Bank also gives importance to Human Resource Development. It has HRD department both at Corporate and Divisional levels. This department conducts training and development courses to its employees. Vysya Bank has training college at Bangalore and Hyderabad.

Views of the Management of Vysya Bank :

The management of Vysya bank is more positive while responding to the aspect of development of human capabilities. On an average, they are positive to an extent of around 0.77. Their opinions are recorded in Table 7.3.

Table 7.3 : Views of Vysya Bank Management on Utilization of Human Capabilites

Management's Views about the Utilization of Human Capabilities	*Weighted Average Value*
Opportunity to participate in management	0.70
Appropriate use of potentialities on job	0.85

Source : Primary Data

Regarding participative management, management feels that they do provide an opportunity to employees to participate in the management. They are positive to an extent of +0.70.

Management is more satisfied with the level of usage of human potentialities on job. They opined that the usage is upto 85% which is fair.

Views of the Employees of Vysya Bank :

Employees of Vysya bank however, contradict management in their opinions regarding improvement of human capabilities. Their opinions are quantified in Table 7.4.

Employees of Vysya Bank are more than satisfied with the

Table 7.4 : Views of Vysya Bank Employees on Utilization of Human Capabilites

Employees' Views about the Utilization of Human Capabilities	*Weighted Average Value*
Opportunity to learn new skills on job	1.14
Job making use of existing skills	0.51
Consultation before any major decision	0.25
Encouragement to participate in management	0.71

Source : Primary Data

opportunity to learn new skills on the job. They are positive to an extent of 1.14.

Interestingly regarding appropriate use of existing skills, employees are not as positive as they are about learning skills. Their job uses their capabilities only to an extent of 0.51.

Consultations of management before any major-decision taken yielded weighted average value of 0.25. Employees could not say that they are satisfied they rated this aspect on positive-side.

One aspect that yielded negative response from employees of Vysya Bank is participative management. Employees expressed that they are not being encouraged at all to participate in the administration of the bank. The weighted-average value of opinions is -0.71.

Trade Union members expressed similar feelings as their counterparts in Andhra Bank. Unions are consulted before any major decision in taken. This is the case only if the decision affects the interests of employees in general. They do not have part in bank administration.

Trade Union of Vysya Bank does not take any measures on its own to improve the capabilities of its members to enable them for promotions. But informal clubs are organised at Branch Level through which periodicals, manuals and other volumes are bought, on mutual interest.

Career Growth and Development

Another important phase of HRD is Career Growth and Development. Each and every employee aspires for an even and fair Career Graph. Bank should assist the employees in reaching higher positions. Bank can help the employe right from planning stage. Career-advancement improves QWL of employee tremendously. As such, the opinions of management of employee respondents and Trade Union members are enquired regarding this aspect. Opinions of management and employees of Andhra Bank in this regard are recorded in Table 7.5 and 7.6 respectively.

Opinion of the Andhra Bank Management :

To start with, management of Andhra Bank has very low level of satisfaction regarding career plan and growth opportunities for

Table 7.5 : Views of Andhra Bank Management on Career Planning and Growth of Employees

Management's Views on Career Planning and Growth	*Weighted Average Value*
Fairness of promotion policy	–0.23
Organisational help in career planning and growth	0.23

Source : Primary Data

employees of their bank. Promotion policy of bank according to them is negative. The ascertained weighted-average value is -0.23.

Regarding career planning and growth they gave similar value as in case of promotion policy on positive side. Here the ascertained value is +0.23. As such on an average management of Andhra bank is absolutely neutral regarding career planning and growth opportunity of employees.

Opinion of the Andhra Bank Employees :

The employees of Andhra Bank are as dissatisfied as the management. For most of the queries they responded negatively. Organisational assistance to their career planning and growth in their opinion is almost nil.

Table 7.6 : Views of Andhra Bank Employees on Career Planning and Growth

Employees' Views on Career Planning and Growth	*Weighted Average Value*
Superior preparing career plans	–0.29
Self preparation of career plans	0.79
Bank providing for career development	–0.03
Employees working towards career development	0.72
Level of satisfaction with promotional chances	–0.86
Level of satisfaction with transfer policies	–0.73
Availability of career counselling facility	–0.69

Source : Primary Data

Employees expressed that their superiors do not plan their career. They are negative in this regard to an extent of –0.29. They responded positively when enquired whether they prepare career plans for themselves. Majority of them felt that this is the case always or sometimes. The weighted-average value ascertained is 0.79.

Similarly, employees expressed that always or mostly they take care of their career development single-handily. As many as 171 of the total sample of 236 agreed to this. Regarding bank's assistance in their career development, employees are almost neutral. The weighed-average value is –0.03.

The employees are mostly dissatisfied regarding chances of promotions in the bank. They rated this aspect at –0.86.

Transfer policy is another policy to bank which incurred the dissatisfaction of employees. The weighted-average value is -0.73.

Management can help employees to draw their career graph by providing counselling facilities. But this facility is not provided by the management of Andhra Bank. For this aspect, employees gave a negative value of -0.69.

As employees are also further enquired regarding various other aspects relating to promotion policy, employees agreed that the basis for promotion is both merit and service. 82 per cent of them also expressed that they get promotion only rarely. Employees personal problems and preferences and constraints are considered now and then by management before transferring any employee. They also expressed that they get promotion only rarely. Employees personal problems and preferences and constrains are considered now and then by management before transferring any employee. They also expressed that they are satisfied regarding management considering their constraints. For example management considers those employees, who spouse is also an employee while transferring.

As almost all employees are Trade Union Members, they also reflected opinions of employees while responding to promotion/ transfer policy. They are sour towards management regarding promotion policy. They felt that bank does not take any measures to graph their career. Politicking also takes place in promotions according to Union members. As such, management, employees and Trade Union members, all agree that the career growth opportunities are at a very low level in Andhra Bank.

The management, employees and trade union members of Vysya Bank have varying view regarding career planning and growth opportunities in the bank. While the management is positive employees and Unions members are mostly either negative or neutral. The opinions of management and employees of Vysya Bank are presented in Table 7.7 and 7.8 respectively.

Table 7.7 : Views of Vysya Bank Management on Career Planning and Growth of Employees

Management's Views on Career Planning and Growth	*Weighted Average Value*
Fairness of promotion policy	0.57
Organisational help in career planning and growth	0.70

Source : Primary Data

Table 7.8 : Views of Vysya Bank Employees on Career Planning and Growth

Employees' Views on Career Planning and Growth	*Weighted Average Value*
Superior preparing career plans	0.21
Self preparation of career plans	1.32
Bank providing for career development	–0.18
Employees working towards career development	0.05
Level of satisfaction with promotional chances	0.00
Level of satisfaction with transfer policies	–0.51
Availability of career counselling facility	–0.59

Source : Primary Data

Sample members of management are either fully satisfied, or neutral. On an average, regarding career planning and development, they are satisfied to an extent of 0.63. They view career development opportunities and promotion policy of that bank as fair. Weighted-average values yield regarding promotion policy and career planning and growth facilities are 0.57 and 0.70 respectively.

Though management of Vysya Bank has a positive picture to present regarding their co-operation in employee's career planning and development, employees are quite dissatisfied. From their opinion presented in Table 7.8, it is observed that employees feel that the bank has no part to play in planning their career.

On the whole, though employees feel that bank does not help them in any way, they are positive to some extent regarding a superior drawing career plans for them. The weighted -average value is +0.21. As many as 44 employees out of total 64 felt that their superior helps them either always, sometimes or now and then.

Contracting this view, they expressed a negative value of -0.18 when enquired regarding bank's part in planning and developing their career. As such it can be assumed that though informally superior helps employees in planning their career, bank officially does not provide any such facility.

Employees quite agree that career plans for them are prepared by themselves and they have to work towards development on their own. As there is no organisational help, employees naturally feel that the whole planning is to be done by themselves. Weighted-average value of opinions are 1.32 and 0.05 respectively.

Employees are absolutely neutral regarding promotional chances available. The average value assessed is '0' which indicates their neutral stand in this regard.

Transfer policy of Bank is another aspect of employee's career to which they respondent negatively. Accordingly to most of the employees 138 out of 641 bank does not follow proper scientific-method in transferring its employees.

Vysya Bank does not provide for career- counselling facilities. Employees are also sour towards this aspect. The weighted-average value assessed is -0.59. As such regarding career-counselling they are more dissatisfied than regarding transfer-policy.

All the respondents expressed that the basis for promotion is both service and merit. They do not get promotions oftens. They also felt that their personal problems, constraints and preferences are considered only if they are very serious or severe. Their problems are considered only now and then.

Members of Trade Unions shared similar views as employees. They are very much dissatisfied with the counselling facility and promotion chances in the bank. Though this aspect did not result in any serious action from Union, it had been a debated topic from quite sometime. On the other hand Unions themselves are not providing any facility for career- planning and development to their members.

Work itself leads to the higher-order needs of employees. After satisfaction of basic needs like monetary/physical and social needs an employee aspires for the development of human resource. Challenging job utilizes human capabilities to full extent and provides opportunity for intellectual satisfaction. As such opinions of management and employees of both the banks are gathered to assess its impact on these parties. The opinions of Andhra Bank management and employees are recorded in Table 7.9 and 7.10.

Table 7.9 : Opinions of Andhra Bank Management on Work and Quality of Work Life

Management's Views on work and QWL	*Weighted Average Value*
Work as a motivational factor	0.20

Source : Primary Data

As far as management is concerned, opinions are collected as to whether work is a motivational factor for employees. Because unless management believes that work is a major motivational factor, they do not take any measures to improve it. Management of Andhra Bank agrees to this argument only to the extent of 0.20. As such they do not attribute much value to this aspect.

As against opinion of management regarding work as motivational factor, employees give more importance to this factor. This trend is evidence from employee's views regarding job-enlargement and job-rotation. Employees of Andhra bank are more than positive i.e., they strongly agree that job-rotation, enlargement and enrichment contribute to the general growth and development of employee. They rated this aspect at 1.35. Same is the case with their views regarding their contribution to the bank.

With job-rotation, enlargement and enrichment they felt that they can contribute more to the bank. The weighted-average value assessed here is +1.11.

Table 7.10 : Opinion of Andhra Bank Employees on Work and Quality of Work Life

Employees' Views on QWL	*Weighted Average Value*
Frequency of rotation among different jobs	0.51
Frequency of enlargements to job	-0.22
Frequency of job enrichent	0.13
Availability of minimum required training to take up enriched/enlarged job.	-0.05
Boredom resulting out of job	-0.86
Part of job-rotation, enlargement & enrichment in general growth of employee	1.35
Contribution with job rotation, enlargement and enrichment	1.11

Source : Primary Data

Regarding the nature of job, employees tend to take mostly neutral stand. Most of them i.e., around 60% feel that their job over-strains their abilities. They also feel that they are usually interested in the job. As much as 73% of the employees agree with the statement that "A job is mainly a way of making money but should be satisfying if possible". While 20.5% of them feel that job is whole way of life, it is only 6.5% of employees who felt that job is only a way to make enough money. This trend shows the importance that Andhra Bank employees attribute to nature of work.

Since job rotation, enrichment and enlargement are important factors which make one's job challenging and interesting opinions of employees are also gathered in this regard.

Employees felt that they are rotated among jobs sometimes and not often. According to employees job enlargement in past ten years were only rare. The weighted-average value yielded is -0.22. Regarding the frequency of their job enrichment, majority of them i.e., 84 employees felt that enlargement are either often or sometimes and 66 of them feel it is now and then.

Minimum required training is received by employees mostly now and then. Employees also strongly disagree with the statement that they get simply with their job. As many as 168 employees out of 236 disagree with this statement, whereas 32 of them take neutral stand. As such management and employees have contradictory views to present regarding conduct and the nature of job.

The management of Vysya Bank attributes negative value to the work as a motivational factor, while 3 managers felt that work does motivate an employee. As a result, this trend resulted in a negative value i.e., -0.28. The views of Vysya Bank are presented in Table 7.11

The views of employees of Vysya Bank are also gathered and

Table 7.11 : Opinion of Vysya Bank Management on Work and Quality of Work Life

Management's Views on QWL	*Weighted Average Value*
Work as a motivational factor	–0.28

Source : Primary Data

recorded in Table 7.12. From the table, it is observed that employees of Vysya Bank attribute importance to the nature and content

Table 7.12 : Opinion of Vysya Bank Employees on Work and Quality of Work Life

Employees' Views on QWL	*Weighted Average Value*
Frequency of rotation among different jobs	0.96
Frequency of enlargements to job	0.05
Frequency of job enrichent	0.42
Availability of minimum required training to take up enriched/enlarged job.	0.37
Boredom resulting out of job	–0.62
Part of job-rotation, enlargement & enrichment in general growth of employee	1.63
Contribution with job rotation, enlargement and enrichment	1.39

Source : Primary Data

of job as against their management. Employees are positive and strongly agree to the extent of 1.63 that job rotation, enlargement and enrichment help in employees general growth. Employees also felt that job enrichment, enlargement and rotation help them in contributing more towards the bank than what they do at present. The assessed weighed-average value is 1.39.

Employees of Vysya Bank have more or less similar views as their counterparts in Andhra Bank have, regarding nature of their job. Around 72% of the employees expressed that they are usually interested in their job. Around 77% of them agree to this statement. Almost entire sample i.e., 59 out of a total sample of 64 employees felt that, a job is mainly a way of making money but should be satisfying, if possible.

Regarding job rotation, enlargement and enrichment employees of Vysya Bank are more satisfied than those of Andhra Bank. The weighted average value ascertained is +0.96 for frequency of job rotation. However, weighted-average value is +0.05for frequency of job enlargements. The frequency of job-enrichments are more than enlargements. This is quite evident form the ascertained weighed-average value 0.42 in case of job-enrichment. Employees also felt that sometimes they receive training before taking up an enriched/enlarged job. Employees strongly contradicted the statement that they simply get bored with their job due to the routine nature of job. As many as 35 employees out of 64 disagree with the statement, while 12 of them felt that it is the case now and then.

As such employees of Vysya Bank contradict the views of their management regarding work as a motivational factor which is turn improves Quality of Work Life.

Organizational-structure is another important factor which contributes towards Human Resource Development thereby affecting Quality of Work Life. Various levels of managements, their span of control, and communications network operating in the organisation are all the factors which affect Human Resource Development.

As such an attempt is made to find out the structure of both the banks. An attempt is also made to find out the opinions of management and employees of both the banks regarding appropriateness of their organisational structure and its effect on their work-life. The expressions of management and employees of Andhra bank regarding organisational structure are presented in Table 7.13 and 7.14 respectively. Opinions of management and employees of Vysya Bank regarding the same are presented in Table 7.15 and 7.16 respectively.

Table 7.13 : Feelings of Management of Andhra Bank Towards Organisational Structure

Feelings of Management towards Organisational Structure	*Weighted Average Value*
Level of satisfaction with communications network.	0.18

Source : Primary Data

Table 7.14 : Feelings of Employees of Andhra Bank Towards Organisational Structure

Feelings of Employees towards Organisational Structure	*Weighted Average Value*
Fairness of relations between line and staff eployees	0.91
Level of satisfaction with comunication network	0.55
Feelings regarding too many bosses	–0.29
Feelings regarding less number of subordinates	0.25
Feelings regarding lack of authority	0.40

Source : Primary Data

Table 7.15 : Feelings of Management of Vysya Bank Towards Organisational Structure

Feelings of Management towards Organisational Structure	*Weighted Average Value*
Level of satisfaction with communications network.	0.57

Source : Primary Data

Table 7.16 : Feelings of Employees of Vysya Bank Towards Organisational Structure

Feelings of Employees towards Organisational Structure	*Weighted Average Value*
Fairness of relations between line and staff eployees	–0.18
Level of satisfaction with comunication network	–0.09
Feelings regarding too many bosses	0.34
Feelings regarding less number of subordinates	–0.23
Feelings regarding lack of authority	–0.03

Source : Primary Data

Managements are enquired mainly regarding communications network available in the bank as this is the most important factor of organisational structure. The management of Andhra Bank is positive regarding their satisfaction about communications network available in the organisation only to the extent of 0.18. Majority of 43 managers felt that communication-network in their organisation is satisfactory to some extent. They avoided to choose two extremes i.e., they neither say that it is superb or it is worse. They tend to take mostly neutral stand.

Employees of Andhra Bank on the hand are generally satisfied with the communications network available in the organisation. They are positive towards this aspect to the extent of +0.55. They also expressed that the communication regarding any policy decision is received through formal communication.

Relations between line and staff employees is satisfactory according to a majority of employees. The weighted-average value assessed here is +0.91. Employees also disagree to the statement that they have too many bosses. The negative weighted-average value assessed here is -0.29. As many as 106 employees of the total sample agree to the statement that they believe that they can manage more subordinates than those they have at present, while 70 employees neither agree nor disagree. Andhra Bank employees aspire for authority to some extent along with accountability. This is evident from their acceptance of the statement that they only have accountability but not authority. The positive average value assessed here is +0.40.

As such management and employees of Andhra Bank have two different views to present regarding significance of communication-network and organisational structure.

Employees of Vysya Bank are dissatisfied regarding various aspects of organisational structure including communication network, inspite of management is concern for communication network. In fact, management of Vysya Bank is satisfied regarding communication-network available in the organisation to the extent of 0.57. As such management of the Bank is fairly satisfied with the network.

Employees of Vysya Bank on the other hand, are dissatisfied with the available communications network. They expressed that only formal communication is followed to spread any policy decision. They are also dissatisfied regarding communication-network in the organisation to the extent of -0.09. Employees are also dissatisfied regarding the relations between like and staff employees. They are dissatisfied to the extent of -0.18 in this regard.

Employees of Vysya Bank have contradictory views to present regarding span of control compared with those of their counterparts in Andhra Bank. To start with, they do agree to the statement that they have too many bosses. They attributed positive value +0.34 to this aspect. However by attributing a negative average value of -0.23 they indicate that they cannot manage more subordinates than that they have at present. Employees are mostly neutral regarding level of accountability and authority. They neither agree nor disagree to the statement that they only have accountability and not authority. Weighted-average value ascertained is 0.03 which is close to neutral value '0'.

Employees of both the banks are dissatisfied with the measures taken by the management to develop human resource. Though managements expressed their satisfaction regarding understanding the significance of HRD, they fail to practice HRD in its true spirit.

As far as utilisation of human capabilities is concerned, though management and employees of both the banks are positive, management and employees of Vysya Bank are more satisfied than their counterpart in Andhra Bank. On an average management of Andhra Bank is satisfied to the extent of around 0.55, whereas management of Vysya Bank is satisfied to the extent of around 0.77.

Employees of Andhra Bank are on an average satisfied to the extent of 0.38 and that of employees of Vysya Bank to the extent of 0.65. The difference of level of satisfaction between these two groups is especially evident in case of encouragement to participative management and opportunity to learn new skills.

In case of career-planning and development also, management and employees of Vysya Bank are little more satisfied that their counterparts in Andhra Bank. Management of Andhra Bank is quite negative towards the promotional policies of the bank whereas management of Vysya Bank is positive to the extent of 0.57. As such top management may take necessary step to reorganize promotional policies of the bank.

Employees of both the banks agree that there is meagre or no help from superiors in planning and/or development of their careers. Hence they view that they themselves have to plan and develop their careers. Though employees of Vysya Bank feel that career-plans are self-made, they are also positive to the extent of 0.21 regarding superiors preparing career plans. As such it may be assumed that this help is informal. Regarding transfer policy and career counselling facility, employees of both the banks are clearly negative. Regarding promotional policy, while employees of Andhra Bank are quite dissatisfied, employees of Vysya Bank are neutral. As such both employees and management of Andhra Bank realise the inferior promotional policy. As such, it is felt that this aspect should attract immediate attention of top management.

In case of work and Quality of Work Life as part of Human Resource Development, Vysya Bank altogether fails to recognize significance of this aspect, whereas management of Andhra bank is positive to the extent of 0.20. Employees on the other hand clearly recognize the significance of nature and content of work as motivational factors. Employees of both the banks are positive regarding practising job rotation, enlargement and enrichment which are important factors to make one's job interesting and challenging.

Job rotation and enrichment are practiced in both the banks, though frequency is more is case of Vysya Bank. Regarding the practice of job enlargement, employees of Andhra Bank are negative whereas employees of Vysya Bank are close to neutral. Employees of both the banks agree that they do not experience any kind of boredom in their jobs.

As such management of Vysya Bank should realise that challenging work as such contributes towards Quality of Work Life and strive towards improving it. Inspite of the absence of management's commitment towards improving content and nature of work, employees of Vysya Bank are more satisfied with their jobs.

As part of Human Resource Development, reaction of management, regarding the level of satisfaction with communications network are recorded. Management of Vysya Bank is satisfied more than half of positive value 1, whereas Vysya Bank employees feel negatively towards this aspect. This trend continues even in case of relations between Line and Staff employees. While Andhra bank employees are perfectly satisfied, employees of Vysya Bank attribute negative value to this aspect.

As far as span of control is concerned, Vysya Bank employees are positive to some extent that they have too many bosses, while Andhra Bank employees disagree. On the other hand, Andhra Bank staff is more content than their counterparts in Vysya Bank, towards authority provided along with accountability.

On the whole, from the opinions of management and employees of both the banks it can be concluded that utilisation of human capabilities and career planning and development opportunities are more in Vysya Bank than Andhra Bank. In case of work, motivational factor and organisational structure, Andhra Bank has a better picture to present. However, this is only a comparative study. Nowhere does the management and employees of any bank fully satisfied and contended.

Human Resource Development is an important phase of Quality of Work Life especially in case of organisations like Banks where each and every employee has a minimum formal education. As such managements have to take steps in those areas where they are lagging behind.

Trade Unions also, though aware of less efforts from management's side to develop human resource, are not taking any measures to improve the same. Trade Unions also can take up HRD programmes by way of arranging lectures, seminars and other development programmes.

Note :

1. P. Subba Rao, op. cit.

8

Evaluation and Suggestions

Introduction

Human Resource Management assumes more importance today as it has never before. Human Resource makes difference and has an everlasting impact on survival of an organisation. Many organisations prospered with the realisation of importance of human resource. Among three M's i.e., money, men and machines, Men are more complex and important. As against other factors of production, human resources do not normally depreciate.

In fact, with good organisation and motivation human resource develop its potential. Although human resource is a subsystem of the total system i.e., organisation, it affects all others subsystems and entire organisation in turn.

Human Resource Management consists of many subsystems like training and development, compensation, industrial.

Most of the industrially developed countries are practicing QWL with better results. United States of America is the pioneer of the concept. Richard E. Walton, an American Professor played major role in developing the concept QWL. The experience of Quality of Work Life in General Motors yielded excellent results. Later QWL was introduced in other major organisations of USA, like Ford and Chryslov and American Telephone and Telegraph Company (AT & T). Many Federal agencies and private organisations are working towards spreading and developing the concept QWL.

United Kingdom also contributed considerably towards the practice of QWL. Toustock Institute of Human Relations carried out research into socio-technical system from which QWL emerged, Shell U.K. Ltd., in its Microwave department to overcome impending labour problem, KI to improve sales levels introduced QWL into their organizations. These programmes produced good results to these organisations.

In Sweden also, where management reserves a right to 'hire and fire' and 'distribute and manage jobs', steps had been taken to redesign jobs and make workers participate.

Italy has been rise and fall of QWL practices. But now again the Government realised the significance of this

The eight point criterion of Walton to measure QWL include—(1) Adequate and fair compensation, (ii) Safe, healthy working conditions, (iii) Opportunity to develop human capabilities, (iv) Opportunity for career growth, (v) Social integration at work place, (vi) Constitutionalism, (vii) Work and quality of life, and (viii) Social relevance.

Apart from Walton's eight point criteria, Klatt, Mudrick and Schumster identified 11 specific issues in general. They are: (i) Pay and stability of employment, (ii) Occupational stress, (iii) Organisational health programmes, (iv) Alternative work schedule, (v) Participative management and control of work, (vi) Recognition, (vii) Superior-subordinate relations, (viii) Grievance procedure, (ix) Adequacy of resources, (x) Seniority and merit in promotion and employment and (vi) Employment on permanent basis.

Genesis of Andhra Bank and the Vysya Bank Limited

Banking industry is a very important tool in the economic building of any country. Banks provide wide range of financial services. In developing countries, banks also discharge social responsibilities like uplifting the weaker sections and financing social projects.

The evaluation and growth of banking industry can be reviewed in two stages:

1. Pre-Nationalization (prior to 1969)
2. Post-Nationalisation (1969 onwards)

Though banking industry has its roots ever-since 1688 in India it is only after 1939 that the industry has achieved subsistence after initial setbacks and failures. As result of policy of Reserve Bank of India to encourage scheduled banks and partition of country during 1947, many individual banks have come up in place of indigenous banks. Reserves Bank of India was established as the Central Bank of the country under Reserve Bank of India Act, 1934. There were also multiple amalgamations and liquidations during this period which resulted in rapid decline in the member of both scheduled and non-scheduled banks.

Social control was imposed on banks on 14th December 1967 to make banking system serve our socio-economic objectives. Two steps were taken to impose social control. One is setting up of National Credit Council and secondly, enactment of Banking Laws (Amendment) Act of 1968. The subsequent failure of social control forced Government to take extreme step of nationalisation of 14 major commercial banks.

As a result of nationalisation, banks opened their branches especially in rural areas. The advances extended to priority sectors also increased considerably. Changes take place in the list of priority sectors from time to time. But agriculture takes prime share from total advances.

Genesis and Growth of Andhra Bank

During struggle for independence, freedom fighters like Pattabhi Seetharamiah thought of fighting for a separate state. As part of this they came up with many regional institutions. The call of Father of Nation, Mahatma Gandhi also stressed the need for national institutes. In those circumstances Andhra Bank was established at Machilipatnam to cater to the needs of people of Andhra which would be managed by Andhras by Pattabhi Seetharamaih. Andhra bank started its actual functioning from 28th November, 1923. Andhra Bank had to face many teething problems like inculcating habit of banking among general public, appointment of directors, Great Depression, failure of major South Indian banks, Two World wars and resultant depression. All these problem rocked Andhra Bank in its initial stages.

Inspite of the setbacks, the growth of Andhra bank was very rapid in both physical and economic terms. The Andhra bank was started with initial capital of Rs. 1,00,000 which increased to Rs. One Crore in 1975 and the Capital of Andhra Bank increased to Rs. 40 crores in 1990.

Branch expansion in Andhra Bank steadily grew at a slower pace initially and then rapidly. In 1951, Andhra Bank was operating with 50 branches. The total number of branches increased to 931 in 1985, and 1055 in 1889-90.

The staff of Andhra Bank are divided into three categories viz., Officer, Clerical staff and Subordinate staff. Andhra Bank which operated with just three members of staff initially had 10,000 employees in 1983-84. By 1991 the number of employees increased to 15,604.

Andhra Bank was made the lead bank for five districts in the Country viz., Guntur, West Godavari, East Godavari, Srikakulam and Ganjam. Andhra Bank also sponsored two regional banks viz., Rishikulya Grameena Bank in Ganjam district of Orissa and Chaitanya Grameena Bank in Guntur district of Andhra Pradesh.

Genesis and Growth of the Vysya Bank Ltd.

The Vysya Bank, which had its humble beginning in 1930 is the largest private sector bank in the Country today in terms of number of branches, employees, deposits and advances. The founder Chairman of the bank was Margapuram Chengaih Chetty.

The bank had a slow and steady growth in early years. In the years 1971 to 1980 the bank went through a phenomenal expansion in terms of size and resources. In 1984 and 1985, the bank slowly surged from its position as number four to number one in private sector.

The bank got status of a schedule bank in 1948. It started a training college in 1938. The bank has undergone tremendous transformation in last decade. The growth in terms of profits, exports credit etc., is phenomenal.

The bank also has a full-fledged international division to carry out the business on modern lines. Vysya Bank is the only private sector bank which has the membership in the 'Society for Worldwide Inter Financial Tele Communication (SWIFT)', which will help to enhance speed in international transactions.

The Vysya bank was incorporated with an initial capital of Rs. 30,00,000/-. There was a steep growth in 1945 with continued growth of deposits, advances and branches in further years till 1980's. During eighties and nineties there was a rapid increase of deposits, profits and advances.

Need for the Study

With the established importance of human resources in developing countries like India, steps should be taken to develop such human resources by adopting various new techniques like HRD and developing QWL. Improvement of QWL is particularly important in service-oriented organisations, like commercial banks.

Though there are many research works carried on in the area of HRM, there are only a few studies carried on especially on QWL. Studies on QWL in commercial banks are rare to find.

In view of the significance of the study on Quality of Work Life' in commercial Banks and dearth of studies in this area, it is felt that there is a greater need to carryout the study.

Objectives of the Study

The objectives of the study are:

1. To enquire into the economic and employment aspects of quality of work life in Andhra Bank, a public sector bank and The Vysya Bank Ltd., - a private sector bank.
2. To study the quality of work life in terms of social aspects in Andhra Bank and The Vysya Bank Ltd.,
3. To evaluate QWL in terms of development of human capabilities, career-planning and development, nature of work, organisational structure etc., in Andhra bank and The Vysya Bank Ltd., and
4. To evaluate the practices of QWL in Andhra Bank and The Vysya Bank Ltd., and Offer suggestions for improvement of QWL in both the banks, in particular and in the banking industry, in general.

Methodology and Sampling

To attain the said objectives, a detailed study has been undertaken on 'Quality of Work Life' in commercial Banks. In view of the limitations of the resources and common nature of commercial banks, one public-sector bank i.e., Andhra Bank and one private-sector Bank i.e., The Vysya Bank Ltd., are selected for the study.

Required data is collected from - Secondary and Primary sources. Secondary data is collected from Annual Reports of both the banks, Reserve Bank of India Bulletins, records of the Indian Institute of Bankers, Bombay, National Institute of Bank Management, Pune etc. Information is also gathered from HRD departments at Head Offices, training colleges and libraries of both the banks.

Primary data is collected from sample respondents of management, employees and trade union members, through three types of structured questionnaires. A sample of 1.5% of employees and 2% of managers in both banks are selected on the basis of stratified random sampling technique. Thus a sample of 236 employee respondents from Andhra Bank and 64 employees respondents from Vysya Bank are choosen. A sample of 113 management respondents from Andhra Bank and seven from Vysya Bank are selected.

Opinions of respondents are assessed on a 5 point scale, from which the opinions are quantified based on the values '2' for 'most positive', response, '1' for 'positive response' '0' for 'neutral response', '-1' for 'negative response' and '-2' for 'most negative response'. The total value is arrived at by multiplying the value with the number of responses and after adding them. Average value is arrived a by dividing the total value by the number of respondents of that category.

The present study reflects existing state of QWL in Andhra Bank and Vysya Bank. For measurement of QWL Walton's 8 point criteria is used. In addition to this criteria some other aspects like influence of family and trade unions and organisational structure, which are considered as important were also used. These aspects are classified as economic, physical and social conditions and the extend of human resource development.

The entire study has been presented in eight chapters. Evaluation and significance of the concept-quality of Work Life is discussed in Chapter 1. Evaluation and growth of Andhra Bank and the Vysya Bank ltd., are presented in Chapter 2. Research design of the study is presented in Chapter 3. Chapter 4 discusses Economic Aspects of QWL while Chapter V presents impact of employment conditions and constitutionalism. Chapter 6 deals with the Social aspects of Quality of Work Life and Chapter 7 presents Human Resource Development aspects of QWL. Finally, Chapter 8 presents the evaluation of the study and suggestions.

Economic Aspects of Quality of Work Life

Economic aspects are one of the most important motivational factors for most of the employees. Walton in his eight point criteria to measure QWL placed the economic aspects like salary and other benefits at the first place.

Andhra Bank is a major public sector bank. Its employee strength is 15,604. And salary bill is Rs. 75.77 cores in 1992. The total amount of fringe benefits paid by the bank during that year is Rs. 9.67 crores.

Vysya Bank is the biggest private sector bank. The employees strength is 4,314 and the salary bill is Rs. 11.71 lakhs in 1990-91. Vysya Bank also provides various other fringe benefits to the employees.

The management respondents of Andhra Banks expressed mixed views regarding the ability of management of pay and the present salary levels, whereas the management of Vysya Bank is almost absolutely positive. Andhra Bank management is close to positive value 1 whereas Vysya bank management is positive only to the extent of 28% in case of meeting the needs of employees with the salary.

Regarding other aspects like comparison with other banks and cost of living, management representatives of both the banks expressed more or less positive opinions. Management respondents of both the banks also expressed positive opinion regarding the comparison of their pay scales with other banks.

Employee respondents of both the banks unlike management respondents share similar views. Andhra bank employees are considerably more satisfied than that of Vysya Bank employees regarding the adequacy of the salary to meet the requirements. Vysya Bank employees are mostly neutral regarding total salary-meeting needs. Regarding basic and DA-meeting respective needs, the employee respondents are mostly positive with only a few deviations.

Trade Union members of both the banks have expressed almost similar views as that of employees. This is because almost all employees of banks are union members. As such they are generally satisfied with the monetary benefits. However, they suggested restructuring of pay-scales from time to time.

One aspect where employees of both the banks are most dissatisfied is that of HRA. HRA forms an important aspect of gross salary as it provides for employees a place where they relax and prepare for next day's work. Without this basic requirement employee cannot put in effective work.

Another aspect where employees and management are dissatisfied is that of total salary, meeting all needs of employees. Management respondents of Vysya Bank though express their satisfaction regarding pay-scales offered to their employees compared to employees of their banks, are quite satisfied with total salary to meet all needs of employees. Though, except HRA, they are generally satisfied with other components of salary, when it comes to total salary they express their total dissatisfaction as the employees view the gross-salary as rather than the components. Inspite of higher education and job opportunities, women still mostly confine themselves to home. As such earning members in India have to bear entire expenditure single-handedly. As such employees aspire for higher earnings to meet various needs.

Normally the expenditure to be incurred in urban areas would be more than those of rural areas. In case of Andhra Bank those employees who are placed in urban areas have to bear extra expenditure due to higher cost of living of urban areas as they do not receive any additional amount to meet this extra expenditure. Hence, it is suggested that employees working in urban areas may be provided with additional allowances to meet the increased expenditure.

Change in the way of life is another factor which makes it necessary to earn more on part of employees. Refrigerators, air-coolers and televisions which were considered as luxuries earlier are only confronts today. A comfortable house with good water facility, costly and fancy clothes, which were comforts are necessities today. These changes in pattern of expenditure require changes in pay pattern setup as pointed out by trade-union members of Andhra Bank.

Employees of bank are dissatisfied with their pay-scales inspite of fair fringe-benefits being offered. This clearly shows an urgent need for restructuring of pay-scales. Management of Andhra bank on the other hand is of the opinion that they offer fair salaries to their employees inspite of employee's views that salaries are inadequate. Trade Unions are already putting in efforts to take this point to the notice of management. management should reach at a settlement with unions and take steps to implement it as salary as possible as monetary aspect is the most important component to improve QWL and motivation of employees.

Working-Conditions

Working-conditions is hygiene factor. It does not motivate the employees, but its absence causes grave dissatisfaction. Physical working-conditions are for e.g., lighting, water, sitting facility etc. At the outset they may seem negligible, but bad working conditions result in dissatisfaction among employees. Physical working-conditions assumes importance as employee spends 8 hours of the day at his work-place.

Banks are service organisations where physical working conditions assumes more importance as employees have to constantly deal with customers with good cheer and reasoning. Comfortable sitting position, good lighting and ventilation, sufficient rest duration to relax are all the factors which keep the employee in good spirit throughout the day.

As such important components of physical working-conditions are chosen and level of satisfaction are ascertained from all three parties i.e., management, employees and members of trade unions.

Andhra Bank and Vysya Bank do not maintain any separate account especially for physical working conditions. They add upto this expenditure to general expenditure account. However. It is ascertained from personnel/HRM departments at head Officers of banks that both the banks spend around twenty per cent of total expenditure on buying new furniture or maintain already existing employment conditions.

Management of Andhra Bank is mostly positive regarding rest duration they provide to employees and other working conditions constituting employment conditions. Management of Andhra Bank is especially quite satisfied with various physical working-conditions they provide. Weighted average value assessed here is +0.95. Management of Vysya Bank also expressed similar views as their counterparts in Andhra Bank. While they are absolutely positive regarding the rest they provide, they are very close to satisfaction regarding physical working-conditions.

Employees of these banks on the other hand express their dissatisfaction regarding other working-conditions Andhra Bank employees did not complain about the tire-some work whereas Vysya Bank employees clearly expressed that they are tired after a day's work. These views of employees of Vysya Bank contradict the opinions of management who are absolutely positive in this regard.

Employees of both the banks are negative towards canteen, sports and lunch-room facilities. Andhra Bank employees are especially negative towards-Air cooler/Air conditioners facility while Vysya Bank employees are especially negative towards-transportation facility. The order of preference of employees very depending upon the nature of their job, region and life-style. Provided nature of work is similar between employees of both the banks, their preferences can be attributed to other factors.

Though the employees of both the banks are dissatisfied with availability of all physical facilities, they are most negative towards canteen, lunch-room and sports facility. Bank employees are usually very busy during bank hours. Both the banks do not maintain canteen at branch and at all division/zonal level. As such employees get beverages from outside hotels through attendants. There are no lunch-rooms provided by banks. Employees have to have any refreshments at their seats which is not in accordance with the Indian culture. Many employees pointed out in informal discussions that they cannot relax during bank hours until lunch-breaks. If canteen or lunch-room facility is provided they can take a short-break of ten minutes and relax. They also expressed that after this kind of break from work, they can start their work afresh.

Hence, it is suggested that the banks should provide at least lunch-room facility in all their offices.

Employees are also most dissatisfied with available sports facility in spite of annual reports of both the banks proclaiming that they encourage sports. Some of the employees of both the banks felt that encouragement is only at higher levels. Rural and semi-urban branches do not have any such facilities.

Sports and games can integrate whole staff. Management can also organise annual inter-bank or intra-bank sports meets. All these facilities do not cost much for the management.

Trade unions also can take certain measures in this regard. Trade union of Vysya Bank can arrange vehicles for conveyance of employees of basis of contribution from all those who use this facility. This reduces individual costs of employees. Trade unions can also arrange picnics and tours for employees which not only recreate them but also help in the interaction among employees. Involving all employees in such recreational programmes helps in building inter-personal relations among the entire staff.

Walton has given the second most important place to working-conditions among various factors of QWL. But, employees of both the banks are most negative towards this aspect. As such, any kind of effort from either management or trade unions towards improvement of working-conditions will be much appreciated by employees.

Social Aspects of QWL

"Man is a social animal". Social aspects play an important role in the life of any human being. Social system is a complex set of human relationships interacting in many ways. Social-life and work-life of an employee are inter-dependent. Varying roles that a man plays in his social-system influences his work-life. Good quality of work-life requires positive co-ordination and interaction of all these roles.

Social aspects influence QWL in four important ways. One is social integration/inter-personal relations. Employees share their experiences, problems, opportunities, etc., at work place with their superiors and subordinates. The second aspect is social relevance of job. The social status he enjoys outside and the respect his job commands in his social groups are naturally interactive. The third part of social aspects is influence of other institutions like family and trade unions. The demands of employees family and trade unions affect the work-life of employees tremendously. The fourth factor is constitutionalism.

Constitutionalism is another factor, lack of which causes dissatisfaction. As the Constitution of a nation protects the basic rights of employees, constitutionalism should also take care of the rights of employees a like without any discrimination, protect from the invasion of privacy and be given a chance to express their views.

Vysya Bank is younger compared to Andhra Bank. It can build 'team-work' which provides a sense of belongingness to its employees. Both the banks strive to maintain constitutionalism in their bank and in turn good inter-personal relations.

Important components of constitutionalism like conflict-resolution mechanism, grievance-procedure etc., are selected and opinions of management and employees are collected.

Management of both the banks are positive regarding the existence of good inter-personal relations. However, Vysya Bank management is more positive than that of Andhra Bank.

Interestingly, employees of both the banks are more positive than managements in this regard. Employees of Andhra Bank are fully satisfied whereas employees of Vysya Bank are satisfied to the extent of 65 per cent. Leadership-style in both the banks is democratic. Employees respect and like their colleagues. None of the employees of both the banks expressed any negative attitude towards their colleagues. Employees of both the banks also have chances to mingle and chat with their colleagues.

In spite of employees proclaiming that leadership-style is democratic in their banks, expectations of the boss are always more than what they can contribute. Employees of both the banks are consulted whenever a policy decision is taken which concerns them. Though employees of both the banks are encouraged to give suggestions, Vysya Bank employees are neutral regarding their management accepting suggestions given by them. Regarding relations with boss and subordinates, Andhra Bank employees are satisfied whereas Vysya Bank employees felt that their boss unnecessarily interferes in their work.

An interesting phenomena is that employees of both the banks are more positive regarding social integration than their management. Comparatively Vysya Bank management scored higher value of satisfaction and it is the employees of Andhra Bank who are more positive. But both the parties in both the banks are generally satisfied and social integration in both the banks is said to be moderate. Cordial relations among management and employees exist according to employees. This is remarkable achievement on part of both the banks.

Banks image in society, challenging job etc., are the components of social relevance which influence one's job. Employees of both the banks are found to be more than satisfied regarding most of these components. They agree that they put in useful work to the society. Their social status has improved after joining the bank. Their job also secures dignity and respect in society. Employees of both the banks also are proud to talk about their job outside the banks. Vysya Bank employees feel that the social status their job hold is such that their relatives are envious towards their job. Andhra Bank employees, however, are negative to this particular aspect.

Though both the groups of employees are generally proud of the social status that their jobs held with their banks, Vysya Bank employees are more positive. Vysya Bank employees express complete satisfaction with weighted average value +0.98. Andhra Bank employees are positive to the extent of 0.68.

Family is another important social institution. Demands of family affects work life of employees. Positive correlation between family and work life is very important requirement for good quality of work life. Employees of both the banks are moderate regarding coordinating their dual roles.

Most of the employees of both the banks felt that on an average, sleeping time apart, they spend about 6-8 hours exclusively with their family. This is more than what a family asks for in modern day's busy life. Employees of the both banks neither think of nor carry their work to home. Vysya Bank employees do face complaints from their spouses that they cannot stand family expectations due to their jobs. These complaints ought to be attributed to other factors because when employees spend as much as 6-8 hours they can fulfil much of the expectations of family. On the whole, it can be concluded that there is a good balance between family and work-life of employees of both the banks.

The next and very important part of social aspect is trade unions. Influence of unions on employee's work life, their attitude towards management and colleague is especially more in the two banks under study as almost all employees are members of unions. A positive correlation between their dual roles as union members and employees is much required.

The management of Andhra Bank views that unions put in good effort to improve monetary benefits and working-conditions of employees. They are mostly neutral regarding unions part in improving inter-personal relations. Management reacted negatively regarding union's effort in career-development and implementing participative management schemes. As such it can be concluded that the employees feel basic or first order needs and put in an effort to improve them whereas they completely neglect higher-order needs like developing human capabilities and human resource development. Management of Vysya Bank, however, is satisfied with the role played by trade unions in this regard. Management of Vysya Bank is fairly positive regarding all components of QWL except establishment of inter-personal relations. Trade unions failed to put in any effort to improve inter-personal relations. Vysya Bank management seems to be more satisfied regarding union's role in the improvement of QWL.

The views of employees of Andhra Bank coincide with their management. They do put in good efforts to improve monetary and working-conditions aspects of QWL. Regarding constitutionalism, employees are mostly neutral. Improving social aspects of QWL by improving inter-personal relations also draw a positive response but this is negligible. On the whole, the unions of Vysya Bank put in more efforts to improve QWL in the bank.

As far as constitutionalism is concerned both the banks have official procedures to follow but, management mostly encourages its employees to solve their grievances or conflicts informally at branch-levels. In Andhra Bank joint-consultative committee for officers cadre and industrial relations committee for Award Staff are formed at zonal level to deal with conflicts of employees. In Vysya Bank employees can take their conflicts to the committee deal with them. But employees can go up to corporate office only if they cannot reach at a solution at branch and at divisional level.

Handling grievances is done by branch managers at branch level informally in both the banks. Only if solution is not found the mater will be forwarded to zonal/divisional levels and finally to corporate office. Vysya Bank constituted a separate committee for this purpose with an informal group consisting of Deputy General Manager, General Manager, Officers (Personnel).

Privacy of employees is protected in both the banks. They are at no point of time asked to furnish their personal matter after their recruitment.

Management and employees of the banks are fairly satisfied with various components of social aspects. Both the parties expressed their satisfaction with little deviations. Regarding social integration, employees expressed that the expectations of management are always more than their actual contribution. This phenomena can also be considered positive. Mild stress is always desirable.

Employees of both the banks are satisfied with the image of their banks among the public. There is also balance between family and work life of employees. Regarding the other part of social aspect i.e., influence of trade unions, though management and employees of Vysya Bank are positive, the same is not the case with Andhra Bank.

Trade unions of Andhra Bank strive to improve compensation and employment conditions. They put in their maximum effort to improve these aspects. Trade unions are neutral regarding improving inter-personal relations, which imply that they accept and appreciate the policies of management, but do not take any initiative to improve them. Finally, regarding HRD aspects viz., developing 'human capabilities and career growth, the effort of trade unions is nil.

As such trade unions of Andhra Bank are still striving for betterment of basic necessities like monetary benefits and employment conditions. They do not concern themselves with improvement of HRD aspects. Though their effort for betterment of employment conditions is appreciable, they cannot do much regarding pay-scales as banks have prescribed norms to follow regarding this aspect. Also employees are fairly satisfied with the available pay scales. As such trade unions at this stage, have to concentrate on improvement of HRD aspects, which is much required for their career growth and development. Properly planned career party and development of human capabilities accordingly is what is much required. Based upon these requirements, trade unions can also decide training context and they themselves can arrange developmental programmes.

As neither employees or members of trade-unions failed to relate HRD aspects and role of unions, it is the responsibility of management to educate them in this regard. This can be done initially through informal way i.e., by way of informal chats with union leaders, and at later stages formally, through class-room training. Trade unions and management of Andhra Bank are thus suggested to take steps towards improving HRD aspects of QWL.

On the whole, social aspects of QWL can said to be fair in both the banks except role of trade unions on QWL of Andhra Bank employees. Both the banks maintain appreciable level of social image and inter-personal relations.

Human Resource Development Aspects

Human resource is the total sum of knowledge, skills, creative abilities, talents, aptitudes, values and beliefs. Enhancement of utilisation value of human resource depends upon improvement of these aspects.

After fulfilling basic monetary and physical needs, employee look forward satisfying their psychological needs and developmental needs. Improvement of creative abilities, capabilities and knowledge of human resource is more important in service organisations where the very nature of functioning requires all these qualities of employees. Enhancement of these qualities leads to better QWL of employees, by providing the employees to raise to the occasion and satisfy the needs like sense of achievement and accomplishment.

Andhra Bank and Vysya Bank Ltd., have HRD cell at corporate and regional/divisional offices, which carry on various functions of HRD. Both the banks have training colleges which cater to the needs of employees from time to time. Chances for human resource development in both the banks are measured in terms of opportunity to develop human capabilities, opportunity for career growth and development, work and QWL and organisational structure.

The management of Andhra Bank is contented to the extent of 55 per cent with the opportunity they provide to employee to develop human capabilities by way of participative management and utilising their capabilities on job which is moderate. The management of Vysya Bank, however, is more positive (i.e., around 77 per cent) in this regard.

Employees of both the banks contradict their management views with regard to the participative management. Andhra Bank employees are neutral whereas employees of Vysya Bank are clearly negative towards managements' view regarding encouraging the participation in management. Regarding other means of improving human capabilities like learning new skills, using full potentialities on job, management consultation of employees of both the banks are on positive side.

Another important phase of HRD is career growth and development. The management and employees of Andhra Bank fall on the same line in expressing their dissatisfaction regarding career plan and growth facility. They view that promotional opportunities are bleak, transfer policy is not fair and management do not have any part to play in planning for careers of employees. There is no career-counselling facility available in the bank. Management of the bank express its dissatisfaction whereas the employees are negative.

The management of Vysya Bank claims that it provides fair opportunities to employees for career-planning and growth, whereas employees express negative view in this regard. Employees are negative regarding promotional chances in bank.

Nature of job itself inspires human resource. As such challenging work is important to develop human resource. But the management of Andhra Bank agree to this statement only to the extent of around 20 per cent. As such management of Andhra Bank fails to relate nature of work as an important component of QWL. As against this, employees attribute much value to the nature of job. Job rotation, enrichment and enlargement are much needed for effective work according to them. Though job-rotation and enrichment were there now and then, enlargements were rare to find. They are neutral regarding minimum required training before taking up new job. Training in such cases is mostly on job. However, they are never bored while on job and the job overstrains their potentialities to some extent.

Management of Vysya Bank is totally negative to the view that the nature of work itself is a motivational factor. Employees of Vysya Bank express almost similar feelings as their counterparts in Andhra Bank regarding significance of nature and contents of work and training they receive. However, frequency of job enrichment, enlargement and rotation is more in case of Vysya Bank than in Andhra Bank. Though management does not realise the significance of these aspects of job, this is being done as an administrative routine. Frequencies of enrichments and rotations are more than enlargements. Since most of the employees of both the banks feel that their job overstrains their capabilities, managements understandably cannot practise much enlargements. As such employees and managements of both the banks express contradictory views regarding significance of nature of job improvement of QWL.

Various factors of organisational structure like properly designed communications network, span of control, and relations between various layers of management influence the psychological aspects of QWL.

While management of Andhra Bank is satisfied regarding communications network only to some extent, employees are moderately satisfied. Employees also express that there are positive relations between line and staff employees. But they express that they have only accountability and not authority to some extent. They also express that they manage more subordinates than what they have at present.

While management of Vysya Bank is more satisfied with available communications network in the bank than their counterparts in Andhra Bank, employees are negative towards this aspect. The negative attitude of employees continues with regard to other components of organisation structure like span of control. They feel that they have too many bosses and they cannot control more subordinates than what they have at present. Regarding relations between line and staff employees are dissatisfied to the extent of -1.8 per cent.

On the whole, both the banks do not have a satisfactory picture to present regarding human resource development aspects of QWL. The management and employees are in a better position as far as developing human capabilities is concerned. But regarding participative management both the groups of employees are dissatisfied. As such there is an urgent need in both the banks to introduce participative style of management. As managements consult employees on the matters pertaining to them, they can gradually increase this participation level. Regarding career-development also both management and employees of Andhra bank are dissatisfied. Management can take immediate steps to restructure them. Employees of Vysya Bank are also dissatisfied in this regard while management does not realise any need for it. Though bases for promotion are both merit and experience, employees of Andhra Bank feel that politicking takes place. Vysya Bank employees are sour towards transfer policy. Transfers are always inconvenient for employees.

Nature of work is another area where both managements in general expressed negative view. It is interesting to note that in spite of management's absence of commitment towards improving contents of job, employees of Vysya Bank are more satisfied with the nature of their jobs. As such, with due effort in this direction Vysya Bank should make their employees more committed towards their jobs. Management of Andhra bank also should try to increase frequency of job rotation and enrichment in their banks.

Regarding organisational structure again, employees of Vysya Bank are very sour whereas Andhra Bank has a moderate picture to present. Employee's dissatisfaction especially in the areas of relations between line and staff communications network and span of control are undesirable. As such quick action is required by management of Vysya Bank to restructure their organisation.

Human resource development is an important phase is QWL and managements of both the banks are required to take necessary steps to improve wherever they are logging.

Trade unions of the banks also are not taking any steps to improve the situation in the bank. Trade unions of both the banks can especially take steps to improve human capabilities by arranging their own training classes, supplying books and organizing seminars etc. Hundred percent membership of employees makes their task more feasible.

Conclusion

Based upon the opinions of management respondents and employees and members of trade unions, an attempt is made to suggest few measures to all the three parties.

1. Employees of Andhra Bank are most dissatisfied with the Human Resource Allowance provided to the employees. As such management of Andhra Bank should take steps to improve HRA especially for the employees in Urban and sub-urban areas.
2. Though employees of both the banks and especially Vysya Bank employees are dissatisfied with almost all physical working-conditions, managements of both the banks may consider to improve minimum facilities like lunch-rooms and sports facilities etc.
3. Both management and employees of Andhra Bank are dissatisfied with role played by 'Trade Unions in the improvement of QWL. The unions should realise the importance of QWL and strive towards its improvement. Especially trade unions can take steps to develop human resource by way of arranging seminars and lectures etc.,
4. Andhra Bank employees are dissatisfied with promotion policy and Vysya Bank employees regarding transfer policy. Employees of both the banks are also largely dissatisfied with managements cooperation in their career-development. As such managements of both the banks can provide career-counselling facilities to the employees to guide them in their career-advancement.

Bibliography

Arthur Lewis, *The History of Economic Growth*, George & Allen Unwin Ltd., London, 1965.

Bell, C.R., *Men at Work*, London, Allen and Unwin, 1974.

Bideman, A.D. and Drury, T.F., (Eds.) *Measuring Work Quality for Social-Reporting*, New York, Halstead Press, ...

Byrne, D., *An Introduction to Personality*, Prentice Hall, 1966.

Cherns, A, *Using the Social Sciences*, Roulledge and Vegan Paul, London, 1979.

Douglas McGregor, *The Human side of Enterprise*, Tata McGraw Hill Publishers, New Delhi, 1960.

Drucker, P.F., *The Practice of Management*, Allied, New Delhi 1970.

Edwin, B., Flippo. *Principles of Personnel Management*, McGraw Hill Kogakusha Ltd., Tokyo, 1976.

Emeny F.E. and Thorsurd, E. *Form and Content in Industrial Democracy* London, Tovistock, 1969.

Hackman, J.R. and Lloyd J.S., *Improving Life at Work*, Santa Monica, ca: Good-year Publishing Co., 1977.

Keith, Davis, *Human Behavioiur of Work*, Tata McGraw Hill Publishing Company Ltd., New Delhi 1981.

Klatt/Murdick/Schuster, *Human Resource Management*, Charles E. Merrill Publishing Company, Columbus, Ohio, 1985.

McGregor, D., *The Human Side of the Enterprise*, McGraw Hill, New York 1960.

Meir Diswvery Gerold M. & Baldwin Robert. E. *Economic Development Theory, History and Policy*, John Wiley and Sons, New York, 1967.

Michael J. Jucius, *Personnel Management*, D.B. Taraporewals Sons & Company (P) Ltd., Bombay, 1977.

Oliver Sheldon *Philosophy of Management*, Prentice Hall Englewood Cliffs, 1923.

Rudrabasavaraj, M.N., *Dynamic Personnel Administration-Management of Human Resources*, Himalaya Publishing House,Bombay 1979.

Sangeetha, Jain, *Quality of Work Life*, Deep & Deep Publishing House, New Delhi-19.

Subba Rao, P., *Principles and Practice of Bank Management* Himalaya Publications, Bombay, 1988.

Subba Rao, P & Ms. Anita, *Stress Management*, in *Organisational Stress*, Edited by Srilatha et al, Discovery Publishing House, New Delhi, 1991.

Subba Rao, P & Rao, V.S.P. *Personnel/Human Resoruce Management*, Konark Publishers Pvt., Ltd.,

Terry L.Leap & Michael D.Crimo *Personnel/Human Resource Management*, Maxwell Macmillan International Edition.

Tripathi, P.C., *Personnel Management*, Ed, Archana Printers, 1985.

Vroom, V.H., *Work and Motivation*, New York, Wiley, 1964.

Wendell, L. French, *The Personnel Management* Honghton Mifflin Company, Boston, 1978.

Studies

Baldev R. Sharma, *Human Resource Management in Banking Industry*.

Taylor, J.C., *An Emperical Examination of the dimensions of Quality of Working Life*, Centre for Quality of Working Life, Institute of Industrial Relations, University of California, Los Angels, 1977.

Articles

Ahmed, N., *Quality of Work Life: A need for understanding, Indian Management*, V.20(11), 1981.

Alderfer, C.P., *Improving the Quality of Work Life: Group and Intergroup Design*, Washington, U.S. Department of Labour, 1975.

Arya, P., Nature and Extent of Worker Participation in Decision-Making, *Indian Journal of Industrial Relations*, 16(1), 1980.

Baker, S.H. and Hanson. R.A., Job Desing and Worker Satisfaction: A challenge to Assumptions, *Journal of Occupational Psychology*, 48, 1975.

Beer M. and Dricoll J.M., *Improving the Quality of Work Life: Strategies for change*, Washington D.C., Dept. of Labour 1975.

Bennett, S.N., and Blundell, D., *Quantity and Quality of Work in Rows and Classroom Group Educational Psychology*, 1983, Vol. 3(2).

Bhardwaj, S.B.L., *QWL, Perspectives, Dreams and Realities*, Paper presented at National Symposium on QWL, Hayderaba,d 1983.

Boisveri, P., *The Quality of Working Life: An analysis*, Commerical de montreal, FEb. 1977, Vol. 30(2)

Boisvert, M.P., *The Quality of Working Life: An analysis*, Human Relations, 1977, 30(2).

Boisvert, M and Theriault, R., *Importance of Individual Differences in Interventioin and Design for Improving Quality of Working Life*, Commercial De Montreal, 1977.

Brown, D.R., *A Quality of Working Life Model*, The Labour Gazette, 1978.

Butteriss, M., *The Quality of Workinig Life: The Expending International Scene*, Work Research Unit, London, 1975.

Carlson, H.C., *QWL in General Motors in Personnel*, by Miller E.C., 1978.

Cooper, C.L., *The Quality of Managerial Life—The Stresors and Satisfiers*, Advanced Management Education, 1980.

Curle Adam, *Some Aspects of Educational Planning in Under Developed Areas*, Harward Businees Review, Vol.3, Summer. 16. Daniel, W.W., Automation and the Quality of Work, New Society, May, 1969.

Dalta G.D., *Improving Quality of Work Life, Some selections and Concrete Experience*, paper presented in the workshop on Quality of Work Life, National Labour Institute, New Delhi, 1976.

David A. Buchman and David Boddy, *Advanced Technology and Quality of Working Life: The effect of computerised control on biscuit making operations*; Journal of occupational Psychology, 1983, 56(2).

David Bargal, *Occupational Welfare as an aspect of QWL*, Labour and Society, 1982.

Davis. L.E., *Quality of Working Life. National and International Development*; Industrial Relations Research Association, 1977.

De,N.R., *Some Dimensions of Quality of Working Life*, in proceedings, of National Seminar of Quality of Working Life, Bombay, 1976.

De.N.R., *Interlinkage between QWL and QL•*, Productivity, 1982, 22(4).

DSouza, K.C. *QWL: An Evolutionary Perspective*, Abhigyan, Autumn, 1984.

Emener, W.G., and Stephens, J.E., *Improving the Quality of Working Life in a changing (Rehabililation) Environment*, Journal of Rehabililation, August, 1982.

Friendlander, F. and Newton, M. *Multiple impact of Organisaional Climate and Individual Value system upon job satisfaction, Personnel Psychology*, Vol 22, 1969.

Ganguly D.N. and Jaseph, S.S. *Quality of Working Life: Work Prospects and Aspirations of Young Workers in Air India*, Bombay, Central Labour Institute, 1976.

Gass, J.r., Education, *Work and the Quality of Life*. The OECK Observer, (67), Dec. 1973.

Graver, R.F., *AT & T's QWL Experiment. A Practicle Case Study*, Management Review, June, ` 1983.

Greenberg, P.D. and Glaser, E.M., *View points of Labour Leaders Regarding Quality of Work Life Improvement Programmes*, International Review of Applied Psychology, April, 1981.

Guest, R.H., *Quality of Work Life Learning from Terry Town*, Hardwar Business Review, July-Aurust, 1979.

Gupta, S., QWL: *Some Issues in the Indian Context*, Econ. and Politicl Weekly, Vol. 20 (48) No. 30, 1985.

Halley, W.H. and Field H.S. et.al., *Negotiating Quality of Work Life, Productivity and Traditional Issues: Union Members Preferred Roles of their Union*, Personnel Psychology, Summer, 1981, Vol. 34(2).

Irving Bluestone, *The Union and Improving the Quality of Work Life*, Atlanta Economic Review, 1974, 24(3).

James, L. Bowditch and Anthony F. Bruno, *Is the Quality of Working Life Improving*? Studies in Personnel Psychology, 1974, 6(1).

Jinckins, D., *QWL-Current Trends and Direction*, Occasional paper No. 3, Ontario QWL Centre, Toranto, 1981.

Johnson, Carl P., Allexander, Mark and Kabin, *Quality of Working Life: The Idea and its application*, Canada, Ministry of Labour 1978.

Kanungo, R.N., *Work Alienation and the Quality of Work Life: A Cross cultural Perspective*, Indian Psychologist, April 1982.

Karlam S.K. and Ghosh S., *Quality of Work Life: Some Determinants*, Indian Management, Sep. 1983.

Loviz, E. Davis., *Enhancing the Quality of Working Life: Developments in the United States*, International Labour Review, 1977. 116(1).

Maccoby M., *Helping Labour and Management Setup Quality of Work Life Programme*, Monthly Labour Review, March, 1984.

Manga, M.L. and A.Maggu., *QWL: A Study of Public Sector in India* ASCI, Journal of Management, 19(2), 1981.

Mehtam P., *Rising Aspiratioins, Quality of Life and Work Organisation, Productivity*, 22(4), 1982.

Mehta, P., *Rising Aspirations, Quality of Life and Work Organisation*, paper presented at National Seminar on Improving QWL At N.P.C., Delhi, 1982.

Mirvis, P.H., and Lawler, E.E., *Accounting for the Quality of Work Life*, Journal of Occupational Behaviour, July 1984, Vol. 5(3).

Naoler, D.A. Lawlerm E.E., *Quality of Work Life : Perspective and Direction*, Organisational Dynamics, Win, 1983, Vol. II(3).

Peterson. M.F., et. al., *Study of a Quality of Work Life Programme: Organisational Control Experience, Influence and Objective Involvement* Group and Organisation Studies, Dec. 1982, Vol. 7(3).

Ronney, J.M., *QWL in the Office*, Training and Development Journal, April 1982, Vol. 36(4).

Ramesh Gell: *Quality Circles Application to Banking*, in Human Resource Development in Banks, by Anil K. Kandawal, Oxford and IBH Publishing Com., (p) Ltd.,

Rosow, J.M., *Quality of Working Life and Productivity - The Double Pay Off*, A paper presented in work in America Institute Conference, Chicago April, 1977.

Rosow J.M., *Quality of Work Life-Issues for the 1980s*, Training and Development Journal, March 1988.

Rice R.W., *Organisational Work and the Overall Quality of Life*, Applied Social Psychology Annual, 1984, Vol. 5, 155.

Sayeed and Parkash, *The QWL is Relation to job Satisfaction and performance in two organisations*, Managerial Psychology, 2(2), 1981.

Seashere Stanley, E., *Job satisfaction as an indicator of the Quality of Employment*, Social Indications Research, 1974, 1(2).

Seashore Stanely, E., *Assessing the Quality of Working Life - the U.S. Experience*, Labour and Society, 1976, 1(2).

Sekaran, V., *Perceived Quality of Working Life in banks in Major Cities in India*, 8, Prajanan, Vol. 14(3), 1981.

S.Sharma Baldev R., *Industrial Democracy - The Indian Experience*, Vol, 22 No. 3, Jan. 1987.

Singh J.P., *Improving QWL in Indian Context*, Productivity, Vol. 22(4), 1982.

Singh, P., *Motivational Profile & Quality of Corporate Work Life; A Case of Mismath*, Indian Management, Feb. 1984.

Sinham J.B.P., *The QWL in Indias Setting*, Journal of Social and Economic Stutides, 5(2), 1976.

Sondhi, S. and G. Bhardwaj, *QWL in the Indian industrial Scene: A Myth or Reality*, Indian Psychological Review, 1986, Vol. 31.

Subba Rao, P., *Bank Branch Manager as Counseller*, State Bank of India Monthly Review, Vol XXV No. 10, Oct. 1986.

Thamos G. Cummings, Molloy and Edwards., *Improving Productivity and the Quality of Working Life*: Praeger Special Studies, New York, 1977.

Thorsrud, *QWL in the First and Third World*, Productivity, Vol. 22(4), 1982.

Udai Pareek, *Introducing HRD in Banks in Human Resource Development*, Anmol Publications, New Delhi.

Walton, R.E., *Criteria for the Quality of Working Life, in the Quality of Working Life*, Vol-I by Davis, L, et. a., London, The Free Press 1977.

Walton, R.E., *Ideas for action. Improving the Quality of Work Life*, Harward Business Review, May-June, 1974.

Westley, W.A., *Problem and Solutions in the Quality of Working Life*, Human Relations Reb. 1979, Vol. 32(2).

Index

Adam, Curle 47
Ageavold 14
Ahmed, N. 52
All India Bank Employees Association 65
All India Bank Officers Conference 65
Andhra Bank
—, Genesis and Growth 35-40 126-28
—, Views of Management of 62-64
—, Attitude of Employees 64-67
—, Employment Conditions in 73
—, —, Management Views 73-74
—, —, Employees' Views 74-76
—, Social Integration, Management Views 85
—, —, Employees Views 85
—, Balance Between Family and Work Life, Management Views 94
—, —, Opinion of Employees of 94
—, Balance Between Trade Unions and Work Life, Management's Point of View 97-98
—, —, Employees' Point of View 97-98
—, Constitutionalism in Bank, Opinions of Management 102-02
—, —, Employees' Views 102
—, Development of Human Capabilities, Opinion of Management of 106-07
—, —, Opinion of Employees 107-08
—, Career Growth and Development, Opinion of the Management 110-11
—, —, Opinion of Employees 111-12
Andhra Bank Award Staff Employees Union 65
AT & T 13, 25

Banking Industry, Post-Nationalisation Development of 32-35
Banking Laws (Amendment) Act of 1968 31
Bharat Lakshmi Bank 37

Carlyle 3
Central Bank of India 28
Cherns 9
Chetty Mengapuram Chengaiah 40

Chetty, Pamidi Subbarama 41
Chetty, Suryanarayana 41
Chrysler 12, 125
Cooper, C.L. 52
Craver, Robert F. 4

D. Souza, K.C. 52
Dayal and Sharma 15
De 6, 49
Desai, Morarji 31
Drucker, Peter F. 2

Emery and Thorsurd 10, 21

Fayol 7
Fiat 14
Ford 12, 125
French, Wendell L. 3
Friedlander, F. 52

Gandhi, Mahatma 35
Gelli, Romesh 50
General Motors 12
Greve, R.F. 52
Guest, Robert H. 4, 52

Herzberg 8
Human Relations Movement 8-9
Human Resource Development, Aspects of 140-44
Human Resource Management, Significance of 47-48

IBM 14
IDBI 62
IFCI 62
Imperial Bank 36
Indian Institute of Management, Ahmedabad 53
Industrial Disputes Act 1847 20
Italidev 14

J & K Bank Ltd 42

Karla, S.K. and S. Ghosh 52

Lahiri and Srivastava 15
Lewis, Arthur 1

McGregor 2, 8-9
Maccoby 51
Maslow 8-9, 19, 72
Mehta 51
Meier and Baldwin 47

NABARD 62
Nadler and Lawler 5
Nationalisation of Banks 31
National Labour Institute, Delhi 53
Newton, M. 52

Olivetti 14

Pareek, Udai 51
Philips 14
Proctor and Gamble 14

Quality of Work Life Past and Present 3-8
QWL—India—Abroad 10-17
QWL Measuring 17-21
—, Barriers to 23-26
—, Sepecific Issues of 21-23
—, Significance of, in Service Oriented Industries 49-50
—, Social Aspect of 135-40

Reserve Bank of India 28, 42
Reserve Bank of India Act 1934 28
Rice, A.K. 9, 11
Rosow 4, 48, 51

Seashore, Stanley E. 51
Seetharamaih, Pattabhi 35, 37
Setty, S. Gopala Krishna 41
Setty, S.V. Sreenivasa 41
Sharma, Baldev R. 50

Sheldon, Oliver 2
Shell U.K. Ltd 13
Singh, J.P. 51
Singh, P. 51
Sinha and Sayeed 51
Socio-Technical System 9-10
Sri Krishnadevaraya University 53
Subba Row, P. 50

Tavistock Institute of Human Relations 9, 11, 13, 126
Taylor, F.W. 6-7, 49
Taylor, J.C. 51
Thorsrud 15, 51

University of Calcutta 53

Vysya Bank, Genesis and Growth of 40-43, 128-29
—, Future Plans 43
—, Management's Perception 67-68
—, Employees' Views 69-71
—, Employment Conditions 76-77
—, —, Management' Attitudes 78
—, —, Employees' Attitudes 78-82
—, Social Integration, Opinions of Management of 88
—, —, Views of Employees of 88-90
—, Social Relevance of Work, Views of Employees 91-93
—, Balance Between Family and Work Life, Opinion of Employees of 94-95
—, Balance Between Trade Unions Work Life, View Point of Employees of 98-101
—, Constitutionalism in Bank, Management about 102-03
—, —, Employees' Views 103-04
—, Development of Human Capabilities, Views of Management of 109
—, —, View of Employees of 109-10
—, Career Growth and Development View of Management 113
—, —, Employees' Views 113-24

Walton, Richard 4, 12, 17, 19, 48